Generis
PUBLISHING

Wine Legislation in Italy

Geographical Indications, Oenological Practices and the Impact of European Reform

Francesco Tedioli
Giordano Zinzani. Stefano Senatore
Vanni Fusconi, Ludovica Elena Asia Colombo

Title: Wine Legislation in Italy

Geographical Indications, Oenological Practices and the Impact of European Reform

ISBN: 979-8-89966-118-1

Author: Francesco Tedioli, Giordano Zinzani. Stefano Senatore,Vanni Fusconi, Ludovica Elena Asia Colombo

Cover image: www.pixabay.com

Publisher: Generis Publishing
Online orders: www.generis-publishing.com
Contact email: info@generis-publishing.com

To my father,
whose values and memory continue to guide me.

Editor's Introduction

Francesco Tedioli – Editor

This collective volume was conceived with the aim of providing a comprehensive, scientifically rigorous, and up-to-date overview of the legal framework governing the wine sector, both at the European and national levels. In a historical moment marked by intense regulatory evolution—ranging from the far-reaching reform of geographical indications to the implementation of the new Common Agricultural Policy (CAP) 2023–2027 and the modernization of oenological and labeling standards—the wine sector emerges not only as a strategic economic domain but also as an extraordinarily complex legal field. It intersects with agricultural law, food law, sustainability policies, and intellectual property, thereby offering a privileged lens through which to observe broader developments in EU legal integration.

The structure of the book reflects this multidimensional nature. The first part is dedicated to the European Union's legal framework, with contributions that examine the latest legislative and delegated acts: the revised system of geographical indications (GIs), the new regime for traditional specialities guaranteed (TSGs), the use and labeling of GI ingredients in processed products, the evolution of electronic labeling and traceability requirements, and the legal reception of OIV resolutions within EU law. Particular attention is devoted to the enhanced role of the European Union Intellectual Property Office (EUIPO), as well as to the implementation of new certification and market access requirements for wine products under EU law.

The second part turns to the Italian legal framework, with a series of contributions that analyze, from a national perspective, the legal transposition and operationalization of European wine law within Italy. These chapters address, among others, the civil law profiles of agricultural land loans and agrivoltaic installations, the fiscal treatment of multifunctional farming practices, the national implementation of the CAP strategic plan in the vitivinicultural sector, and the classification of ancillary agricultural activities with specific reference to wine production.

By combining a sector-specific focus with cross-cutting legal analysis, the volume aims to promote an integrated understanding of the normative and institutional dynamics at play. It is designed to be of use not only to legal scholars and academic researchers, but also to practitioners, public authorities, and professionals engaged in the governance and operation of the wine supply chain.

I wish to express my sincere gratitude to all the authors for the quality of their contributions and for the spirit of intellectual collaboration that animated the preparation of this volume. Their work reflects a shared commitment to scientific excellence and legal clarity, which we hope will serve the broader wine law community in the years to come.

Francesco Tedioli

Supreme Court lawyer, expert in agricultural law and Adjunct Professor of Commercial Law at the University of Mantova. He is the editor of this volume and the author of over 100 articles published in national and international journals on agricultural law, agrivoltaics, and agribusiness. Member of the Scientific and Editorial Committee of the journal *Consulenza Agricola*, he regularly contributes to the national and international legal discourse on the regulatory framework governing agricultural and rural activities.

Giordano Zinzani

Oenologist and executive in major wine cooperatives, Giordano Zinzani has participated as a speaker at numerous conferences and seminars across Italy and Europe, contributing technical articles on innovations in oenological technologies. He has served as a wine judge in leading national and international wine competitions and has collaborated on several research projects and trials conducted in the Romagna region, particularly with the University of Bologna, focusing on wine packaging and preservation. He has held the position of President of the Romagna section of Assoenologi and served as a national board member. From 1999 to 2013, he represented the Italian delegation at the Union Internationale des Œnologues based in Paris. He was also President of the *Consorzio Vini di Romagna* for 12 years and board member of other PDO wine consortia. He is an Academic Member of the Italian Academy of Vine and Wine and Corresponding Academic of the National Academy of Agriculture. He is co-author of the volumes: *Sangiovese vino di Romagna: Storia e tipicità di un famoso vitigno e di un grande vino* (2014); *Romagna Sangiovese – Storia e identità di un famoso vino e di un antico vitigno* (2017); *Champagne e Spumanti di Romagna, dal primo Novecento ad oggi* (2018). He is a regular contributor to *ConsulenzaAgricola*, writing on wine law and regulatory developments.

Stefano Senatore

Lawyer specialized in food and wine law, he provides legal advice and assistance to businesses in the sector, supporting them in regulatory compliance, the management of official controls, and litigation. He lectures on food law at the Edmund Mach Foundation in San Michele all'Adige, as well as in university-level master's programs and advanced training courses. He is the author of numerous articles and columns on food law topics published in various industry journals. He is also a member of CeDiSA (Centre for the Study of Law and Science in Agriculture, Food and the Environment) and of UGIVI (Union of Wine and Vine Lawyers).

Vanni Fusconi

Tax lawyer with specific expertise in agricultural taxation, he provides fiscal consultancy to companies and corporate groups operating in the agri-food sector. His professional activity is primarily focused on tax planning, assistance during tax audits, and representation in tax litigation, with a consolidated specialization in issues arising in the context of primary agricultural production, agro-energy, and connected rural activities. He also contributes regularly publishes technical articles on tax law in leading professional journals.

Ludovica Elena Asia Colombo

Lawyer specialized in civil law, agricultural law, and agri-food law, currently practicing at the Food Law Department of LCA Studio Legale. After graduating in Law from the *Università Cattolica del Sacro Cuore* in Milan, she completed her legal traineeship and professional practice at a leading law firm in Milan, developing expertise in agricultural law and the legal framework governing agricultural enterprises. She obtained a Second-Level Master's Degree in Food Law from the University of *Roma Tre*, gaining specialized knowledge of both national and EU food legislation. She also earned a postgraduate diploma in Wine Law from the University of Florence. In October

2023, she collaborated as a legal consultant with the Italian Ministry of Agriculture, Food Sovereignty and Forests (MASAF), within the Department for Competitive Policies, Agri-food Quality, Fisheries, and Horse-Racing, under the supervision of Dr. Scalera. bShe currently practices as a lawyer in the Food Law Department of LCA Studio Legale, focusing on civil and corporate law matters.

TABLE OF CONTENTS

10. **The Concept of "Connected Activities" in the Wine Sector under Italian Agricultural Law**

Vanni Fusconi **(file:** *Fusconi.docx*)

11. ***The Labelling of Wine and Wine Products: Nutrition Declaration and Health Profiles***

Ludovica Colombo (Colombo.docx)

12. Wine Tourism in Italy: A Legal and Economic Perspective on a Growing Sector

Francesco Tedioli file: Tedioli 4 En.docx)

13. **The Legal and Operational Role of Customs Codes in the International Trade of Italian Wine**

Francesco Tedioli (file: Tedioli 5 En.docx)

The Reform of the Geographical Indication System in the European Union: Scope and Objectives

by Stefano Senatore, Lawyer specialized in food and wine law

1. Regulatory Trajectories of Geographical Indications under the EU Food Law Framework

Regulation (EU) 2024/1143 represents a major reform of the European system of geographical indications (GIs), establishing for the first time a unified legal framework for PDOs and PGIs of agricultural and food products, wines, and spirit drinks. This reform effectively consolidates the three previously separate regulatory regimes into a common body of rules.

Far from being a mere formal reorganization of the pre-existing rules, the intervention of the European legislator introduces a number of substantial innovations aimed at the development and strengthening of the sector. Among these, it is worth highlighting:

- the simplification and acceleration of procedures for registration and amendment of product specifications;
- the enhancement of the role of producer groups (in Italy, Consorzi di tutela), to which new management, control, and enforcement powers over GIs have been granted;
- the encouragement of sustainable practices by producers;
- the strengthening of enforcement tools for online protection and domain name disputes;
- the extension of GI protection in international trade;
- the introduction of a stricter regime for the use of GI-labelled ingredients in processed food products.

The new legal framework does not concern only the stakeholders directly involved in the PDO and PGI supply chains. In fact, the introduction of more stringent protection rules imposes a higher level of diligence on any operator marketing foodstuffs, wines, and spirit drinks—whether generic or bearing a GI—in how they present their goods, including online, in order to avoid infringing upon the rights of other GIs and incurring related criminal or administrative penalties.

In light of the above, this article aims to briefly illustrate the key aspects of the new GI protection system introduced by Regulation (EU) 2024/1143, with the goal of promoting awareness of the legal obligations now affecting a broad range of businesses, with particular attention to the wine sector, in keeping with the theme of this volume.

2. The Fundamental Principles of GI Protection: Scope and Innovations

Regulation (EU) 2024/1143 sets out the general rules applicable to all geographical indications, regardless of product category, in its Title II (Articles 5 to 31). These provisions now form the common core of the system, applicable to agricultural and food products, wines, and spirit drinks alike. The Regulation repeals the previously applicable sector-specific regulations, namely: Regulation (EU) No. 1151/2012 on quality schemes for agricultural products and foodstuffs (now fully repealed), Title II, Chapter I, Section II of Regulation (EU) No. 1308/2013 on PDOs, PGIs and traditional terms for wines (now largely replaced), and Chapter III of Regulation (EU) No. 2019/787 on GIs for spirit drinks (also substantially replaced).

It should be noted that, while the new framework harmonises the core rules on GIs, it nevertheless preserves the specific features that have traditionally characterised each of the three product sectors. For instance, the rules on traditional terms continue to apply exclusively to wines, while the scheme for Traditional Specialities Guaranteed (TSGs) remains reserved for agri-food products.

This common set of rules essentially confirms and systematises the criteria already in force, while introducing certain important new elements. Among these, the most noteworthy is the explicit extension of protection to GIs used not only for designating products, but also services. In this way, the EU legislator adopts the approach already developed by the Court of Justice of the European Union, according to which the use of the term *"Champanillo"* as the name of a tapas bar chain (and therefore to designate a catering service rather than a product) could potentially constitute an evocation of the protected GI *"Champagne"1.*

The Regulation also confirms that protection applies to any use of a registered GI that takes advantage of its reputation or exploits its distinctive character. It expressly provides that evocation may occur even in the absence of a risk of consumer confusion, or where the protected GI is accompanied by expressions such as "type", "style", "imitation", or similar wording. These principles had already been affirmed in EU case law and are now codified, removing any ambiguity about their binding nature.

In addition, the legislator clarifies the concept of *"comparable products"*, stating that this status may exist even in the absence of an identical category classification. This reflects the position taken by the Court of Justice, which held that—under the criteria in force—all spirit drinks, though falling under different product categories, are to be regarded as comparable. Consequently, the use of the term *"Cognac"*—a registered GI for category 4 ("wine spirits")—was deemed unlawful when used in a trademark referring to products in category 33 ("liqueurs")[2].

3. Online Market Protection of Geographical Indications

As previously mentioned, the recent reform aims to ensure that the rights associated with geographical indications (GIs) are fully safeguarded in the context of online commercial activities. The protection measures set out in Article 26(1) of Regulation (EU) 2024/1143—concerning unlawful commercial use of names, misappropriation, imitation, evocation, and other misleading indications or practices—are now explicitly extended to cover:

14. Distance sales, including e-commerce (Art. 26(4)(b));
15. Domain names (Art. 26(2));
16. Online intermediary services (Art. 43(1)), a category that encompasses a wide range of services involving the electronic transmission or storage of information, including search engines and e-

1 Court of Justice of the European Union, 9 September 2021, Case C-783/19, *Comité Interprofessionnel du Vin de Champagne v. GB.*

2Court of Justice of the European Union, 14 July 2011, Joined Cases C-4/10 and C-27/10, Bureau national interprofessionnel du Cognac v. Gust. Ranin Oy.

commerce platforms, which are now directly involved in the enforcement of GI protection[3].

With specific regard to domain names, the reform introduces additional provisions of significant interest. Notably, Article 42(4) requires each Member State to adopt judicial and administrative measures enabling the removal or disabling of access—from within its territory—to any domain name that infringes GI rights. By way of example, a domain name such as "asolo.it" could be considered evocative of the PDO "Asolo Prosecco" and thus subject to such measures.

As a consequence, Italy will be required to implement dedicated geo-blocking tools for the protection of GIs, enforceable by judicial authorities or designated administrative bodies. It is reasonable to expect that this role will fall to the Italian Communications Authority (AGCOM), given the analogous enforcement powers it already exercises in combating unfair commercial practices[4], fraud, and online piracy[5].

In a complementary fashion, Article 35(1) introduces important changes to the field of alternative dispute resolution (ADR) mechanisms concerning domain name allocation. These mechanisms are currently embedded in the contractual frameworks between domain name registries and their registrants, and they allow third parties—typically trademark holders—to challenge the allocation of a domain name and to seek reassignment when their rights are infringed.

However, existing ADR frameworks have generally been unavailable for asserting rights based on GIs. The reform addresses this gap by imposing a binding obligation on domain name registries to recognise PDOs and PGIs as

---

3The forms of liability and accountability imposed on intermediary service providers are, incidentally, governed by a dedicated set of rules laid down in **Regulation (EU) 2022/2065** (commonly referred to as the **Digital Services Act**).

4 Article 98-decies of Legislative Decree No. 259/2003, as amended by Article 1, paragraph 37 of Legislative Decree No. 48/2024, provides that AGCOM (the Italian Communications Authority), pursuant to its own specific regulatory framework, may order the blocking of domain name system resources accessible from users located within the national territory, in cases involving aggressive commercial practices, fraud, or abuse.

5 For the protection of copyright in the online environment by AGCOM, reference should be made to the dedicated Regulation adopted by Resolution No. 680/13/CONS, as subsequently amended. More recently, AGCOM's powers have been explicitly defined and expanded at the legislative level by Law No. 93/2023, whose Article 2, paragraph 1 grants the Authority the power to order service providers, including internet access providers, to disable access to unlawfully disseminated content by means of DNS resolution blocking of domain names and network traffic blocking directed toward IP addresses specifically assigned to illicit activities.

enforceable rights in ADR proceedings. Nevertheless, this obligation is limited in scope, applying exclusively to registries that:

- Administer country-code top-level domains (ccTLDs), such as ".it", ".es", or ".fr", while excluding generic top-level domains (gTLDs) like ".com", ".org", or ".net";
- Are established within the European Union, thereby excluding registries located in third countries, even when they manage ccTLDs.

In sum, the provisions outlined above demonstrate a clear intensification of control and protection over data published online—whether through corporate websites, e-commerce portals, search engines, or domain names—for the benefit of GI holders. This protection framework, which encompasses both public enforcement mechanisms and private legal remedies, underscores the importance for operators to exercise increased diligence and strategic foresight in managing their digital presence going forward.

4. Protection of GI Ingredients Used in Processed Products

Article 27 of Regulation (EU) 2024/1143 finally introduces a harmonised legal framework governing the conditions and modalities for communicating the presence of PDO and PGI ingredients in processed food products (such as, for instance, a "Romagna" DOC wine used in the dough of a tarallo or in the filling of a biscuit, where the producer wishes to highlight that ingredient on the label or on its website).

This legislative intervention was particularly awaited, as it responded to a widely recognised need for clear and uniform rules in an area that, until now, had been regulated inconsistently—through non-binding guidelines[6], judicial initiatives[7], or fragmented national legislation across the Member States[8].

As a general rule, the EU legislator now allows the name of a PDO or PGI used as an ingredient to appear in the name, labelling, and advertising materials of the processed product, provided that the following three cumulative conditions are

6 Reference is made, in particular, to Commission Communication 2010/C 341/03 — Guidelines on the labelling of food products using ingredients designated as Protected Designations of Origin (PDOs) or Protected Geographical Indications (PGIs), published in OJ C 341/3 of 16 December 2010.

7 In this regard, significant impact was attributed to the judgment of the Court of Justice of the European Union of 20 December 2017, in Case C-393/16, Comité Interprofessionnel du Vin de Champagne v. Aldi Süd Dienstleistungs-GmbH & Co. OHG

8In Italy, for example, the wine sector has developed a specific system for the protection of GI ingredients, which is still governed today by Law No. 238/2016 (the so-called Consolidated Law on Vine and Wine), Article 44, paragraph 9.

met (as already outlined in Commission Communication 2010/C 341/03, cited in note 7):

a) the processed product must not contain any comparable ingredient other than the one designated by the GI;

b) the GI-designated ingredient must be used in sufficient quantity to impart an essential characteristic to the processed product;

c) the percentage of the GI-designated ingredient must be indicated on the label.

An additional condition applies where the name of the geographical indication is to be used in the name of a pre-packed food product, including in its promotional materials. In this case, the use of the GI is subject to a prior written notification to the recognised producer group—a new figure institutionalised by the Regulation and functionally equivalent to the Italian "erga omnes" Consorzi di tutela[9]. The operator may only proceed with use of the GI after receiving a written confirmation of receipt of the notification or, in its absence, after a waiting period of four months has elapsed.

Upon receiving the notification, the recognised producer group may—alongside confirming receipt—also provide non-binding information on the use of the GI concerned. In addition, the parties may enter into contractual agreements specifying the technical and visual aspects of how the ingredient's GI may be presented.

The involvement of recognised producer groups introduced by the new system therefore aligns the EU framework more closely with the Italian experience. However, it should be noted that under Italian law—as set forth in Law No. 238/2016, Article 44(9)—notification alone is not sufficient: the express authorisation of the Consorzio di tutela is required before a protected name can be used.

The national requirement of prior authorisation may, incidentally, be maintained by Italy pursuant to Article 27(2) of Regulation (EU) 2024/1143. Nevertheless, in our view, the national system will need to be adapted—hopefully in the near future—in order to align it with the new European rules.

---

9 In the wine sector, Article 41(1) of Law No. 238/2016 provides that a producer group (Consorzio di tutela) for a PDO or PGI, where it ensures a minimum level of representativeness among winegrowers and certified production, may be authorised by the Ministry of Agriculture, Food Sovereignty and Forests to operate on an erga omnes basis, that is, "in the interest of and with respect to all operators subject to the control system of the PDO or PGI, including non-members."

In conclusion, Regulation (EU) 2024/1143 constitutes a significant step forward in the protection of geographical indications, though it also requires a greater degree of diligence and compliance awareness from all operators in the agri-food sector.

The 2024/2025 Grape Harvest Guidelines: An Overview of Italy's Regulatory Framework for the Wine Sector

By Giordano Zinzani, oenologist and expert in wine legislation

1. Introduction and Regulatory Context

The regulatory framework governing the Italian wine sector is known for its complexity, both in terms of the volume of applicable rules and the multi-level structure of sources, including European regulations, national legislation, and ministerial decrees. In recent years, however, one constant reference point for sector operators has been the annual publication of the *Vademecum vendemmiale*, a comprehensive guide issued by the ICQRF (Central Inspectorate for the Protection of Quality and Fraud Repression of agri-food products), under the aegis of the Ministry of Agriculture, Food Sovereignty and Forests (MASAF).

The guide for the 2024/2025 wine campaign was released at the end of July on the official MASAF website. It provides a detailed yet accessible outline of the principal compliance obligations imposed on wine producers, with direct references to the applicable legal norms and implementation rules.

The 32-page document includes over fifty footnotes referencing ministerial decrees, implementing regulations, laws, and circulars. In addition to its main content, the guide contains a **synoptic table summarising the accompanying documentation required for the transport of wine products**, and a **dedicated appendix**.

2. Structure and Content of the 2024/2025 Harvest Campaign Guide

The 2024/2025 edition of the *Vademecum vendemmiale* is organized into three main sections:

7. **Section I**: This section outlines the primary obligations for wine producers, including the registration of harvest and production declarations, the management of the electronic wine register, and the procedures for the movement of wine products.

8. **Section II**: This part provides a synoptic table summarizing the accompanying documentation required for the transport of wine products, facilitating compliance with traceability and authenticity standards.
9. **Section III**: The final section includes an appendix with detailed explanations of specific cases and scenarios, offering practical guidance for operators in the sector.

The guide is available on the official website of the Ministry of Agriculture, Food Sovereignty and Forests (MASAF) and can be accessed directly through the following link: Vademecum vendemmiale 2024/2025.

3. Yield Limits for Vineyards Producing Generic Wines

Among the various regulatory elements that characterize the Italian wine production system, one of particular relevance for vineyard operators concerns the limits imposed on grape yields per hectare. These yield thresholds serve a dual purpose: they ensure the quality and authenticity of products bearing quality designations such as PDO (Protected Designation of Origin) and PGI (Protected Geographical Indication), and they help regulate the market supply of generic wines, thereby preserving a certain balance between production capacity and economic sustainability.

For vineyards registered to produce PDO or PGI wines, the maximum permitted yields are defined in the official product specifications (*disciplinari di produzione*) approved for each denomination. These specifications may be updated annually to reflect climatic conditions, production expectations, or specific decisions by local Consortia and authorities. In contrast, vineyards not intended for the production of PDO/PGI wines—but nevertheless included in the national vineyard register (*schedario viticolo*)—are subject to a general statutory yield limit.

According to Article 8(10) of Law No. 238 of 2016 (the so-called *Consolidated Wine Law*), as amended by Article 224 of Decree-Law No. 34 of 2020, the maximum yield for such vineyards is set at **30 tonnes of grapes per hectare**. However, a derogation from this general rule has been introduced through a series of ministerial decrees. In particular, the Ministerial Decree of 23 December 2021 and the more recent Ministerial Decree No. 692724 of 18 December 2023 allow for yields of up to **40 tonnes per hectare** in specific municipalities located in the regions of Emilia-Romagna, Molise, Puglia, Veneto, and Lazio.

These derogations are not granted arbitrarily but are based on objective agronomic criteria and socio-economic considerations, such as the traditional productivity of certain territories, the characteristics of local grape varieties, and the importance of viticulture for local rural economies. Thus, the regulatory framework offers a degree of flexibility, while still maintaining an overarching system of controls aimed at ensuring the traceability and integrity of the Italian wine supply chain.

For producers, it is essential to remain updated on any changes introduced through such decrees, as the eligibility for increased yield limits is determined on a municipality-by-municipality basis and may vary from year to year. In this respect, the *Vademecum vendemmiale* serves as a practical and reliable tool for verifying compliance with the current rules.

Type of Vineyard	**Maximum Yield (tonnes/ha)**	**Legal Basis / Conditions**
Vineyards for PDO/PGI wines	As defined in PDO/PGI product specifications	Product specifications approved for each denomination
Generic vineyards (non-PDO/PGI)	30 tonnes/ha	Art. 8(10), Law No. 238/2016
Generic vineyards with derogation	Up to 40 tonnes/ha	Ministerial Decrees (e.g., D.M. 692724/2023); applies to certain municipalities in Emilia-Romagna, Molise, Puglia, Veneto, Lazio

4. Transport Documentation and Electronic Record-Keeping in the Italian Wine Sector

The management of transport documentation and mandatory record-keeping represents a central pillar in Italy's wine regulatory system. These requirements serve both traceability and transparency objectives and are grounded in a harmonized legal framework that incorporates both national and European provisions.

4.1 The Electronic Wine Register (*Registro Telematico Vitivinicolo*)

Since the entry into force of Ministerial Decree No. 293 of 20 March 2015, the keeping of wine production records in Italy must be carried out exclusively via electronic means. The so-called *registro telematico vitivinicolo* (electronic wine register) is administered through the SIAN (Sistema Informativo Agricolo Nazionale), the central IT system operated under the authority of the Ministry of Agriculture (MASAF).

All wine producers subject to this obligation must ensure that their operations—including grape harvesting, vinification, bottling, storage, and transfers—are properly recorded through the SIAN portal: http://www.sian.it/portale-mipaaf/home.jsp. The portal also provides access to technical documentation, operational guidelines, and a comprehensive FAQ section specifically related to the use of the electronic register.

4.2 Simplification Measures and One-Time Notifications

The Italian regulatory system allows certain simplifications for specific cases, in line with the broader goals of digital innovation and administrative streamlining, as promoted under Decree-Law No. 76 of 16 July 2020 (converted with amendments by Law No. 120/2020).

This includes:

17. A **one-time notification** for producers of *mosto cotto* (cooked grape must);
18. A **preliminary communication requirement** for wineries processing or handling musts and wines in facilities where also other non-authorised substances are used, as governed by Article 14 of Law No. 238/2016;
19. Exemptions from prior communications in certain cases (e.g., packaging for direct sale of wines listed under Art. 16 of Law No. 238/2016), provided that the operation is later registered in the electronic system.

These provisions significantly reduce bureaucratic burdens while maintaining a solid framework for compliance monitoring by the ICQRF's territorial offices.

4.3 Mandatory Pre-Notifications and Communication to Control Bodies

Within the SIAN system, a wide range of telematic communications are available—and in some cases mandatory—prior to carrying out specific oenological practices or movements of wine products. In certain situations, these declarations must also be transmitted to the control bodies (Organismi di Controllo) responsible for monitoring compliance with PDO/PGI specifications.

Here is a non-exhaustive list of the most significant mandatory telematic communications:

Type of Communication	**Description**
Production of *mosto cotto*	One-time declaration of cooked grape must production
Temporary storage centers for by-products	Notification of dedicated locations for by-products
Holding of grape marc (vinacce) for alternative uses	Declaration of intended non-distillation uses
Withdrawal of by-products under official control	Required for vinification residues
Use of mixed facilities (*stabilimenti promiscui*)	Communication of processing of wines/musts with other ingredients
Use of chemical substances not authorized in winemaking	Must be declared in advance
Rectified concentrated must (RCM) processing	Advance declaration required
Enological practices involving specific substances	Includes use of potassium ferrocyanide, calcium phytate, DL-tartaric acid
Sparkling wine fermentation (*spumantizzazione*)	Subject to pre-declaration requirements
Use of carbon dioxide	If employed in oenological practices
Yeast preparation and sugar syrup dosage	Especially relevant in sparkling wine production

These obligations are designed to ensure that all critical operations in the wine production chain remain under administrative scrutiny, enabling authorities to verify compliance with both food safety and quality requirements.

4.4 Exemptions from the Obligation to Maintain the Electronic Wine Register

Although the electronic wine register (*registro telematico vitivinicolo*) represents the backbone of traceability in the Italian wine supply chain, the national legal framework provides for certain targeted exemptions, designed to avoid imposing disproportionate administrative burdens on very small operators or those with limited volumes of production.

In particular, winegrowers and winemakers whose total annual production does not exceed **50 hectolitres**, and who operate within facilities where direct sale to consumers or food service activities (such as restaurants or agritourism operations) are also carried out, are not required to maintain the electronic register. For these producers, compliance with record-keeping obligations is instead ensured through the submission of two standard declarations:

- the **production declaration**, to be filed annually and detailing the volume of wine and must obtained during the harvest season;
- the **stock declaration**, which reflects the quantities of wine and must physically present in the winery as of **midnight on July 31** of each year.

A further exemption is provided for **retailers engaged in direct sales to the public**, commonly referred to as *rivenditori al minuto*. These operators are also relieved of the requirement to maintain the electronic wine register, given the limited nature and traceability of their sales.

Such regulatory simplifications reflect a broader principle of proportionality in administrative obligations: they seek to ensure that compliance remains feasible and economically sustainable, especially for small-scale or family-run operations, while preserving the integrity and transparency of the wine market.

5. Stock Declarations and Vintage/Production Reporting: Annual Obligations for Italian Wine Operators

In the context of Italian wine law, two fundamental administrative obligations mark the rhythm of each production campaign: the **stock declaration** (*dichiarazione di giacenza*) and the **harvest and production declaration** (*dichiarazione di vendemmia e produzione vinicola*). These filings are not merely bureaucratic formalities; they form the informational backbone for public oversight of wine production, trade balances, and regulatory compliance.

5.1 The Stock Declaration (Dichiarazione di giacenza)

The stock declaration represents an annual "snapshot" of the volumes of wine and must physically present in a producer's cellar as of **midnight on July 31**. It serves as a closing inventory for the administrative wine year and must be submitted **between August 1 and September 10** through the national SIAN platform.

This declaration excludes any products obtained from grapes harvested during the current vintage, thereby offering an accurate picture of stocks carried over from previous campaigns. Producers who are subject to the obligation of maintaining the electronic register (*registro telematico*) may also use the same system to generate the **annual balance sheet** and to **close the register** as of July 31.

To facilitate compliance, the system is designed to **automatically close** the register if the operator fails to do so manually by the September 10 deadline. This mechanism reduces the risk of non-compliance while ensuring continuity in data collection.

5.2 The Harvest and Production Declaration (*Dichiarazione di vendemmia e produzione vinicola*)

The second key reporting obligation concerns the volumes of grapes harvested and wine or must produced during the current campaign. This **harvest and production declaration** must be submitted **by November 30** of each year and follows a standardized format accessible via the SIAN system.

For operators using the electronic wine register, the declaration process is simplified: the system allows them to **import relevant data directly from their register**, minimizing duplication of input and potential errors.

In support of this process, the Italian Agency for Agricultural Payments (AGEA) issues an **official circular** each year, detailing the procedures and timelines for the submission of harvest and production declarations. The circular typically includes updates on regulatory changes, technical specifications, and operational guidance tailored to the current vintage.

6. Oenological Practices and Fermentation Periods: Regulatory Developments and Compliance Requirements

The European and Italian legal frameworks governing oenological practices have undergone significant updates in recent years, particularly in response to evolving market trends, technological innovation, and public health considerations. For wine producers, awareness of the regulatory landscape in this area is essential, not only to ensure legal compliance but also to preserve the qualitative integrity of their products.

6.1 Applicable Legislation and Recent Amendments

The primary sources of law regulating oenological practices in the European Union are:

- **Commission Delegated Regulation (EU) 2019/934**, which lists the authorized oenological practices and conditions for their use;
- **Commission Implementing Regulation (EU) 2019/935**, which complements the above by providing operational procedures and limitations.

Both entered into force on **7 December 2019**, replacing previous provisions under Regulation (EC) No. 606/2009. These texts have since been updated, most notably by:

- **Commission Delegated Regulation (EU) 2022/68**, which replaced Annex I of Regulation 2019/934, including:
    - **Table 1**: List of authorized oenological practices;
    - **Table 2**: List of authorized oenological compounds.

These amendments, in effect since **8 February 2022**, reflect a more systematic and transparent regulatory approach to the use of additives and processing aids in winemaking.

6.2 Dealcoholization and New Functional Categories

One of the most notable changes was introduced by **Regulation (EU) 2021/2117**, which amended Regulation (EU) No. 1308/2013. Among other innovations, the amendment introduced a formal **legal framework for the dealcoholization** of wine products. This allows producers to reduce the ethanol content of wines partially or almost entirely, responding to growing consumer demand for low- and no-alcohol alternatives.

As of now, however, **Italy has not yet implemented** domestic procedures for the production, storage, or labelling of dealcoholized wines. The Ministry of Agriculture (MASAF) is currently working on specific guidelines to define the conditions under which such products may be lawfully produced and commercialized in the country.

6.3 Acidification and Deacidification Practices

Acidification is another practice regulated under both EU and national law. Producers are allowed to acidify either **grape musts** or **finished wines**, within limits established by European legislation. The general limit is set at **4 grams per litre** (equivalent to **53.3 milliequivalents/litre**) of tartaric acid.

Notably, the law allows:

- The acidification of pre-wine products (e.g., musts or partially fermented musts) even if the original must had already undergone acidification, provided they belong to different categories;
- The acidification of wine itself, even through multiple successive operations;
- Acidification operations to be carried out exclusively within the **same wine-growing zone** where the grapes were harvested.

Regulation (EU) 2021/2117 has simplified the administration of these practices by removing the requirement that acidification be performed only at the original winemaking facility. However, the responsibility for tracking acidification quantities now lies with the operator, including obligations to:

- **Inform downstream buyers** of the acidification data for each lot sold;
- **Keep internal records** and note acidification details in the electronic wine register;
- **Report the aggregate acidification values** when assembling different wine lots.

In practice, the **"codice partita"** field in the electronic wine register must reflect the acidification level (e.g., "acidification 2.5 g/L"), which determines the creation of distinct inventory lots by the system. In case of blending different lots, a **weighted average** must be calculated and recorded.

6.4 Sweetening and Administrative Simplifications

Unlike under the previous regime (Regulation No. 606/2009), producers are **no longer required to submit specific declarations** to the competent authorities before carrying out:

- Sweetening operations;
- Acidification or deacidification practices.

However, it remains mandatory to **record such operations** in the electronic wine register without delay.

6.5 Fermentation Periods and Special Procedures

The official harvest and fermentation period in Italy runs from **15 July to 31 December**. However, exceptions apply in certain cases:

- **PDO/PGI wines**: If permitted by the relevant specifications (*disciplinari*), fermentations may occur outside the standard window, upon notification to the competent ICQRF office;
- **Sparkling wines** (*spumanti*) and **semi-sparkling wines** (*frizzanti*), as well as wines labelled with the traditional term *vivace*, may undergo primary or secondary fermentation in bottles or pressure tanks outside the reference period;
- **Special wine categories**, such as **passito wines** or **non-GI wines**, may be produced under specific timelines, subject to annual authorization by ministerial decree.

6.6 Enrichment Practices (Arricchimento)

Enrichment—meaning the increase of natural alcoholic strength—must comply with the limits and conditions laid down in EU law and **Ministerial Decree No. 278 of 9 October 2012**. Operators may choose among the following methods:

- Addition of **concentrated must (MC)**;
- Addition of **rectified concentrated must (MCR)** in liquid or solid form;
- **Partial concentration techniques**, including **reverse osmosis**.

Operators are allowed to submit one or more **preliminary declarations**, valid for multiple enrichment operations within a defined time period (not beyond 31 December), also through the SIAN portal.

The *Vademecum* includes detailed provisions on the production, transport, and authorized use of MC/MCR.

6.7 Prohibited Substances and Additional Notes

Italy continues to impose restrictions beyond EU law in some areas. For example, under **Ministerial Decree of 21 June 2017**, the use of **oak chips** (*pezzi di legno di quercia*) in the processing, ageing, or refinement of **PDO wines** is strictly prohibited.

Similarly, the use of **paraffin discs impregnated with allyl isothiocyanate**, as a preservative for wine or partially fermented must, is governed by **Ministerial Decree No. 682 of 23 January 2020**.

7. By-products of Winemaking: Legal Requirements, Exemptions, and Alternative Uses

The management of winemaking by-products—such as grape marc (*vinacce*) and wine lees (*fecce di vino*)—is an essential component of Italy's regulatory strategy to ensure both environmental compliance and the integrity of the wine supply chain. These materials, though technically classified as waste or secondary outputs, are subject to detailed legislation that governs their treatment, disposal, or possible reuse.

The key normative reference is **Ministerial Decree No. 185138 of 30 March 2023**, which implements European policy on the **by-product distillation intervention**, with a view to balancing sustainability objectives and administrative efficiency.

7.1 Exemptions from Mandatory Distillation and Controlled Withdrawal

In general, wine producers are required to deliver their by-products to authorized distilleries or to arrange for their withdrawal under official control. However, Article 4 of the above-mentioned decree establishes **exemptions** from this obligation under certain conditions. Specifically, producers are exempt if:

- They process **no more than 6,000 kilograms of grapes** annually; or
- Their total wine or must output does not exceed **50 hectolitres** per campaign.

In such cases, producers are permitted to use alternative methods for managing by-products. However, they must notify the **Ministry of Agriculture (MASAF)**, the **ICQRF**, and the relevant **regional authority** at least **30 days** prior to the first planned withdrawal under control. This communication must include detailed information regarding the intended method of reuse.

7.2 Alternative Industrial Uses and Special Authorizations

Where by-products are destined for **industrial applications** outside traditional distillation (so-called "new industrial uses"), specific authorization is required. In these cases, the Ministry, acting in coordination with the **Customs and Monopolies Agency (ADM)**, may issue permits covering activities such as:

- Non-denatured alcohol recovery;

- Use of by-products in biofuel production or combustion.

These new uses reflect a broader European and national policy goal of fostering circular economy practices in the wine sector.

7.3 Mandatory Telematic Communication and Documentation

For those producers opting to manage their by-products through **controlled withdrawal**, strict procedural rules apply. Operators must:

- Submit a **telematic declaration** at least four days before the withdrawal operation;
- Use the **dedicated SIAN functionality**, which ensures traceability and compliance monitoring.

Importantly, **certificates** issued by distilleries or vinegar factories (*acetifici*) to the producers no longer require prior endorsement or stamping. Instead, the **second copy of the certificate** must be sent via **certified email (PEC)** to the competent ICQRF territorial office immediately upon issuance.

7.4 Deadlines and Storage Periods

Time limits for the removal or delivery of by-products are also regulated by decree:

- **Grape marc (vinacce)** must be delivered or withdrawn within **30 days** after the end of the harvest period (extended to **90 days** for producers under 1,000 hl/year);
- **Wine lees (fecce di vino)** must be handled by **31 July** of the relevant campaign year.

Producers failing to comply within these deadlines may be subject to administrative penalties and sanctions under the national enforcement framework.

7.5 Grape By-products from Table Grapes and Denaturation Requirements

By-products resulting from the processing of **table grapes** are also governed by the rules set out in Ministerial Decree No. 185138/2023. These materials may be destined either for controlled withdrawal or distillation, provided all legal conditions are met.

Of particular note, beginning with the **2024/2025 campaign**, the temporary derogation that allowed the **denaturation of wine lees using sodium chloride** is no longer valid. As a result, all denaturation operations must now use **lithium**

chloride, in compliance with the technical instructions set forth in **Ministerial Decree No. 11294 of 25 September 2017**.

Furthermore, denaturation must always be carried out **before the wine lees are extracted from the cellar**, ensuring that the operation is irreversible and legally compliant.

Requirement / Condition	**Details**
Exemption from distillation	Granted if ≤ 6,000 kg grapes or ≤ 50 hl wine/must/year
Advance notice for alternative uses	At least 30 days before first controlled withdrawal; notify MASAF, ICQRF, Region
Authorized new industrial uses	Subject to authorization by MASAF in agreement with ADM
Telematic declaration for controlled withdrawal	Mandatory; at least 4 days before operation via SIAN system
Certificate transmission	Second copy of certificate must be sent via PEC to ICQRF
Deadline for grape marc removal	Within 30 days after harvest period ends
Extended deadline for small producers (<1,000 hl)	Up to 90 days after harvest for producers under 1,000 hl
Deadline for wine lees removal	By 31 July of the campaign year
Denaturation requirement for wine lees	Must be completed before removal from cellar
Substance for denaturation (2024/25)	Lithium chloride (NaCl no longer allowed)

8. Grape Intermediation Centers and Facilities for the Processing of Table Grapes: Legal Constraints and Compliance Mechanisms

Within the broader legal framework that governs the Italian wine sector, specific attention is devoted to the activities of **grape intermediation centers** (*centri d'intermediazione uve*) and facilities designated for the **processing of table grapes** (*stabilimenti destinati alla trasformazione di uve da tavola*). Although these entities do not engage in winemaking per se, their operations are strictly regulated to ensure that table grapes and their derivatives are not illicitly diverted toward vinification—a practice explicitly prohibited under both EU and national law.

8.1 Scope of Regulation and Risk of Fraud

The regulation of these centers responds to a fundamental concern of the European Common Agricultural Policy: the **separation of supply chains** for table grapes and wine grapes. The potential for fraud—i.e., converting high-yield, low-cost table grapes into wine—undermines both market integrity and consumer protection. It also affects statistical accuracy and may lead to distortions in quota systems and subsidy allocations.

To prevent such risks, Italian legislation imposes a series of **accounting and reporting obligations** on grape intermediation centers and transformation facilities that handle **non-wine grapes**. These obligations go beyond ordinary commercial record-keeping and are designed to ensure that every kilogram of grapes received, stored, and processed is **fully traceable** and **excluded from the wine circuit**.

8.2 Operational and Record-Keeping Requirements

Operators of these facilities must maintain:

- **Dedicated registers** that account for all incoming and outgoing batches of table grapes;
- **Supporting documentation** for all deliveries and product transformations, including the final destination of the processed material;
- **Segregated storage** and handling procedures, ensuring physical separation between grapes intended for wine and those intended for other uses (e.g., juice, fresh consumption, industrial processing).

In addition, such centers may be subject to **random inspections** by the ICQRF and other competent authorities. Violations—whether intentional or due to negligence—can result in the **immediate withdrawal of operational authorizations**, **financial penalties**, and, in more serious cases, **criminal prosecution** under the rules on food fraud.

8.3 Practical Implications for Compliance

Given the heightened scrutiny and regulatory obligations, operators in this segment of the grape sector must adopt a **compliance-first approach** to their business models. This includes staff training, the use of digitized inventory systems where possible, and the regular updating of procedures in line with evolving regulatory interpretations.

For grape growers and traders, awareness of these distinctions is crucial, especially when entering into supply agreements or arranging third-party processing. Contractual language should explicitly address the **intended final use** of the grapes, thereby preventing any ambiguity that could lead to administrative or legal liability.

9. Storage of Grape Musts Below 8% Vol. Alcohol and the Regulatory Framework for Grape Juice Production

One of the less widely known but highly regulated aspects of the Italian wine legislation concerns the **storage and management of grape musts** whose alcohol content is below **8% by volume**. Although such musts may appear innocuous in technical terms, they occupy a sensitive position in the regulatory structure because of their **potential use in unauthorized wine production**.

9.1 Legal Prohibition and Regulatory Objective

Pursuant to **Ministerial Decree No. 944 of 6 September 2017**, it is **explicitly forbidden** to store in wine cellars or oenological establishments any must or wine-related product with an **actual or potential alcoholic strength below 8% vol**, **unless** such product has been duly **denatured**.

The rationale behind this restriction is to prevent the **diversion of low-alcohol grape derivatives**—originally destined for grape juice or industrial use—into the winemaking chain, where they could be fraudulently blended, fermented, or otherwise processed contrary to law.

9.2 Conditions for Lawful Storage of Low-Alcohol Musts

Nevertheless, the law provides a **regulated channel** for the use of these products, particularly in the **grape juice industry**. To lawfully store musts with less than 8% vol. alcohol in oenological facilities, the following conditions must be met:

- The must must be **destined exclusively and definitively** for **grape juice production**, including **concentrated grape juice**;
- The processing must occur at a **different authorized facility** where such transformation is permitted and actually implemented;
- The must must be **transported and handled** in accordance with specific protocols that prevent any contamination or cross-use with wine products.

In such cases, the must does **not need to be denatured** prior to storage, provided that all documentary and logistical controls are in place.

9.3 Mandatory Denaturation in Other Scenarios

Where musts with an alcoholic strength below 8% vol. are instead **processed independently**, without direct connection to juice production or where **distillation is the final use, denaturation becomes mandatory**. This procedure must be carried out **at the time the must is obtained**, using **lithium chloride** or another substance approved by the competent authorities.

The use of **denaturing agents** is a critical safeguard within the regulatory system: it renders the product unfit for human consumption and legally bars its entry into the food and beverage market, thereby neutralizing any risk of fraud.

9.4 Compliance and Control

Operators must keep **detailed records** of all low-alcohol musts entering and leaving their facilities, specifying:

- Alcoholic content;
- Intended use;
- Date and method of denaturation (if applicable);
- Destination facility for juice production.

These records must be made available to the ICQRF and, if required, to the local customs authorities.

Failure to comply with these rules may result in sanctions ranging from **administrative fines** to **suspension of authorizations**, and even **criminal liability** in case of proven intent to circumvent the legal framework.

10. Mixed-Use Facilities and the Legal Framework for Combined Processing Operations

In the Italian wine law system, certain production sites—particularly those belonging to agricultural enterprises or complex processing entities—operate as **mixed-use facilities** (*stabilimenti promiscui*), where **oenological products** are processed alongside other substances or ingredients. This regulatory category is expressly acknowledged and governed by **Article 14 of Law No. 238 of 12 December 2016** (the Consolidated Wine Law), and its correct application is crucial for both compliance and the lawful expansion of production chains.

10.1 Legal Definition and Permitted Activities

A *mixed-use facility* is defined as a wine cellar or processing plant in which operators engage in the **elaboration of products obtained through the use of grape musts or wines**, together with:

- **Sucrose (sugar)**;
- **Wine spirits** (*acquavite di vino*);
- **Ethyl alcohol**;
- Other **substances permitted under Regulation (EU) No. 251/2014**, concerning the definition, description, presentation, and labelling of aromatised wine products.

Such activities are **permitted by law**, provided that the operator **notifies the competent territorial ICQRF office** before each processing cycle. This **advance communication**, which can be submitted **electronically via the SIAN portal**, must be made **per operation**, specifying the type of elaboration and the substances used.

10.2 Notification and Monitoring Obligations

The preventive notification, known as *DPVM* (*Dichiarazione Preventiva di Vinificazione in Stabilimenti Promiscui*), is essential to ensure that regulatory authorities can monitor:

- The **origin and destination of wine-based ingredients**;
- The **quantities** and **types of additional substances**;
- The **integrity of separate production lines**, especially when products are destined for different markets (e.g., wine vs. aromatised beverages).

Failure to submit the required communication may invalidate the operation and expose the operator to administrative penalties or the invalidation of product status (e.g., loss of DOP/IGP eligibility).

10.3 Spirit Drinks and Non-Wine Products in Agricultural Enterprises

Italian law also makes room for **simplified operations in agricultural settings**, where farmers engage in ancillary processing activities. According to **Article 15(4) of Law No. 238/2016**, agricultural holdings (*imprese agricole*) that produce grape must or wine may also:

- Produce **foodstuffs and beverages** listed in Article 15(1), letters b), c), and d);

- Hold and use **aromas, additives, and colourants**, provided such use is consistent with activities considered **functionally connected** (*attività comunque connesse*) under **Article 2135 of the Italian Civil Code**.

In these cases, the law does **not require a prior notification** for processing operations, as long as they fall within the scope of **agricultural connected activities**, meaning:

- Activities directly related to or deriving from the cultivation of the land or the processing of farm-grown products;
- Activities that maintain a functional, organizational, and economic link with the core agricultural activity.

This provision provides **legal certainty and operational flexibility** to farmers who, without moving outside the agricultural sphere, seek to enhance the economic value of their production through modest-scale transformation or diversification initiatives.

10.4 Implications for Labelling and Product Classification

Products derived from processing in mixed-use facilities are **not always classifiable as wine**, especially when additional substances alter their legal and organoleptic profiles. For example:

- Products containing sugar or flavourings may fall under the category of **aromatised wine-based beverages**;
- Mixed alcoholic products may be considered **spirit drinks**, governed by **Regulation (EU) 2019/787**.

Correct labelling and classification are therefore essential not only for consumer information but also for tax, customs, and market access purposes.

11. Sugar Substances in the Wine Sector: Record-Keeping Obligations and Regulatory Distinctions

The use and management of **sugar substances** in the wine sector—both as ingredients and as by-products—are subject to specific regulatory obligations under Italian law. These rules are designed to ensure the **traceability** of all saccharides introduced into the oenological chain, while also distinguishing between different professional figures involved in their production, importation, and use.

11.1 Legal Basis and Scope of Application

The relevant provisions were introduced by **Law No. 12 of 11 February 2019**, a legislative act aimed at simplifying administrative burdens in the agri-food sector. According to this law, the obligation to **maintain sugar registers**—that is, detailed records of the quantities and movements of sugar substances—applies **only to producers and importers** of such materials.

This includes any operators who:

- Manufacture sugar products from raw materials (e.g., sugar beet, cane, or grape derivatives);
- Import sugar, glucose, fructose, or similar substances from third countries or other EU Member States.

In contrast, **wholesalers and end users** (such as wineries or beverage manufacturers) are **exempt** from the obligation to maintain such registers, unless they also engage in production or importation.

11.2 Clarifications on Obligated Parties

The scope of the register-keeping requirement was further clarified by **Ministerial Note No. 5281 of 2 April 2019**, which detailed the professional categories and operational contexts in which the register must be maintained.

The note makes a crucial distinction between:

- Operators who process or sell sugar **as a primary activity**, and are therefore obligated to register each transaction;
- Operators who **merely use sugar** in their production processes (e.g., for fermentation or dosage in sparkling wines), and who are not subject to this obligation.

Such a distinction ensures that compliance efforts are proportionate and targeted, without imposing undue burdens on small or craft producers whose use of sugar is marginal and traceable through other systems (e.g., the electronic wine register).

11.3 Grape-Derived Sugars and the Wine Product Register

Another important nuance in the legal framework concerns **sugars derived from grapes**, such as:

- **Grape sugar** (*zucchero d'uva*);
- **Grape glucose**;

- **Grape fructose**;
- Their **mixtures**.

According to **Ministerial Decree No. 945 of 6 September 2017**, these substances—when obtained from the processing of grapes or musts—are considered **viticultural products** rather than generic sugar commodities. As such, their production and movement must be recorded in the **wine product register**, rather than in the sugar register.

This distinction aligns with the broader principle that **products derived from winemaking raw materials** remain within the regulatory scope of vitiviniculture and are subject to its traceability regime, even when their chemical identity may overlap with industrial or commercial sugar types.

12. Organic Wine Production: Regulatory Framework and Compliance under EU Law

The production of **organic wine** in the European Union is governed by a complex set of rules aimed at promoting environmentally sustainable agriculture, safeguarding consumer confidence, and ensuring the integrity of certified products. Over the past decade, this legal framework has undergone significant revision, culminating in the adoption and full entry into force of **Regulation (EU) 2018/848**, which introduced a uniform regime for all organic food and beverage products, including wine.

12.1 Entry into Force of the New Organic Regulation

Regulation (EU) 2018/848 of the European Parliament and of the Council, dated 30 May 2018, came into full application on **1 January 2022**, replacing the earlier Regulation (EC) No. 834/2007 and its implementing acts.

Under Article 56 of Regulation 2018/848, products obtained in accordance with the previous legislative framework can still be placed on the market **until existing stocks are exhausted**, thus ensuring a transitional continuity.

12.2 Record-Keeping and Input Controls

One of the cornerstones of the organic wine system is the **traceability of inputs**. Pursuant to Article 9 of **Commission Implementing Regulation (EU) 2021/1165**, operators must maintain records of:

- All **products and substances** used in vinification;
- All **cleaning and disinfection agents** employed;

- The **date(s)** of use;
- The **name and active ingredients** of each substance;
- The **location of use**, where applicable.

This comprehensive traceability system serves not only as a compliance mechanism but also as a safeguard for the credibility of organic labels in the eyes of consumers.

12.3 Authorized Inputs and Non-Organic Exceptions

The list of authorized inputs for the **production and storage of organic wine** is contained in **Annex V, Part D** of Implementing Regulation (EU) 2021/1165. These substances must be used:

- In strict accordance with EU sectoral rules, particularly Regulation (EU) No. 1308/2013 (CMO Regulation) and Delegated Regulation (EU) 2019/934;
- Within the limits and under the conditions prescribed for each substance or practice;
- Consistently with any national rules deriving from or complementing EU law.

Notably, **Article 8 and Annex 5** of the Italian **Ministerial Decree of 20 May 2022** permit, under specific circumstances, the use of certain **non-organic products and substances** in the production of organic wines. This provision is designed to ensure the feasibility of production when organic alternatives are either unavailable or impractical.

12.4 Special Case: Use of Grape-Derived Sugars

Within the system of organic production, a specific issue arises regarding the use of **grape-derived sugars**—particularly **rectified concentrated must (RCM)**—in the enrichment or sweetening of organic wines or food products.

According to EU law, only **RCM**, whether in liquid or solid form, is currently permitted to bear the **"organic" designation**, due to the fact that its production method—typically involving ion exchange resins—is explicitly authorized within the organic quality regime **only for vitivinicultural products**.

Consequently, if a food product lists "organic grape sugar" among its ingredients, the producer must be able to demonstrate that the ingredient used was in fact **organic rectified concentrated must**, and **not** another type of sugar derived from grapes but **not recognized** as compliant under the relevant EU organic regulations.

13. Labelling of Wine Products under EU Regulation 2021/2117: New Obligations and Electronic Disclosure

As of **8 December 2023**, producers of wine and wine-based products within the European Union are subject to **new labelling obligations**, introduced by **Regulation (EU) 2021/2117**, which amended Article 119 of the **Common Market Organisation Regulation (EU) No. 1308/2013**. These changes mark a significant step in aligning wine labelling with broader food law, especially in the fields of **consumer information**, **nutrition**, and **ingredient transparency**.

13.1 Mandatory Information on Wine Labels

The amended legislation requires that all wine products placed on the market from the above date must display the following **mandatory particulars**:

- The **nutritional declaration**, either complete or limited to the **energy value**;
- The **list of ingredients** used in the production of the wine;
- For wines that have undergone **dealcoholization** and have an alcohol content below 10% vol., the **minimum durability date** (i.e., best-before date).

These obligations apply to all wines, regardless of their denomination or production method, and extend to still, sparkling, aromatised, and partially dealcoholised products.

13.2 Electronic Labelling Options and Data Protection

In a notable departure from the labelling requirements applicable to other foodstuffs, **wine producers are allowed to limit the physical label** on the bottle to:

- The **energy value**, which may be expressed using the symbol **"E"** (for "energy").

In such cases, the **full nutritional declaration** and the **complete list of ingredients** may be provided **electronically**, via a link printed on the label or packaging.

To ensure consumer privacy and compliance with data protection principles, the regulation explicitly provides that:

- No **user data** may be collected or tracked when accessing such electronic disclosures;
- The link must not redirect to commercial or promotional content, but **only to the mandatory information**.

This innovation aims to strike a balance between transparency and **label space constraints**, particularly relevant for small-format bottles or producers with multilingual markets.

13.3 Allergen Labelling

Regardless of the use of electronic disclosure, **allergen information** must always be stated **directly on the label**, using the word **"contains"** followed by the name of the allergenic substance or product, as listed in **Annex II of Regulation (EU) No. 1169/2011**.

For wine products, the mandatory allergen indications include:

- **Sulfites**: must be declared as "sulfites" or "sulphur dioxide";
- **Eggs and egg products**: "egg," "egg protein," "egg derivatives," "lysozyme from egg," or "ovalbumin";
- **Milk and milk products**: "milk," "milk derivatives," "milk casein," or "milk protein".

In addition to textual declarations, **pictograms** may also be used, as specified in **Annex I, Part B** of **Regulation (EU) No. 2019/33**.

In addition to the textual declaration, producers may choose to display **pictograms** representing the presence of allergens. These symbols—such as those indicating sulphites, eggs, or milk—are listed in **Annex I, Part B** of **Commission Implementing Regulation (EU) 2019/33**. While optional, if used, they must conform strictly to the official models and be clearly visible on the label. It is important to note that the pictogram **does not replace** the mandatory wording "contains [name of allergen]" in the relevant language of the country where the wine is marketed; it may only supplement it.

13.4 Ingredient Nomenclature and Clarifications from the European Commission

The terminology used in the list of ingredients is also regulated. Article 48 bis of **Regulation (EU) No. 2019/33** provides that certain terms—such as "grapes," "concentrated grape must," "sugar syrup," and "dosage syrup"—may be used under precise conditions. Additional rules apply for:

- **Oenological compounds in general**;
- **Compounds with allergenic potential**;
- **Additives and processing aids**.

To assist producers in implementing these complex rules, the **European Commission** published a guidance document titled *"Questions and Answers on the Implementation of the New EU Labelling Requirements for Wine"* in the **Official Journal of the European Union, Series C, on 24 November 2023** (Document C/2023/1190).

13.5 Implications for Transport and Accompanying Documents

The new labelling requirements also affect the **transport documentation** for wine products. According to Regulation (EU) No. 1308/2013, the accompanying documents must include all mandatory particulars required by law, including:

- The list of ingredients;
- The nutritional declaration.

However, in the case of **bottled wine**, these details are considered already available on the label. Therefore, they **need not be repeated** in the transport document, as long as the authorities can reasonably access the same information.

For **bulk wine** (vino sfuso), where space on the transport document may be limited, a separate information sheet may be attached, provided that:

- A reference to the attachment is included in the appropriate section of the main document;
- The attachment itself clearly lists all mandatory particulars.

Mandatory Seals for DOCG Wines, Optional for DOC Wines, and Recently Extended to IGT Wines

By Giordano Zinzani, oenologist and expert in wine legislation

1. Regulatory Foundations for the Use of Seals on DOCG Wines in Italy

In Italy, Article 48 of Law No. 238 of 12 December 2016 — *"Organic Framework on Vine Cultivation, Wine Production and Trade"* **— establishes that wines classified as *Denominazione di Origine Controllata e Garantita* (DOCG) must be released for consumption bearing a special seal (*fascetta*), applied under the responsibility of the bottling companies. This seal is printed by the *Istituto Poligrafico e Zecca dello Stato* (State Printing Office and Mint) or by authorized printing houses and must be affixed in such a way as to prevent its reuse. It includes a serial indication and an individual identification number.**

2. Optional Seals or Batch Identification Codes for DOC Wines: Regulatory Flexibility and Alternative Traceability Systems

The seal is also used for packaging wines classified as *Denominazione di Origine Controllata* (DOC). For these wines, as an alternative to the seal, the use of a "batch identification code" (*lotto*) is permitted pursuant to Article 118 of Regulation (EU) No. 1308/2013, in application of Directive 2011/91. The batch code is assigned to the certified lot by the bottling company and communicated by the same company to the body responsible for the control plan. Thus, the use of seals is not mandatory, except for DOCG wines. Article 48 of Law No. 238/2016 delegates to the protection consortia—or, in their absence, to the regional authorities, after consulting the relevant wine production chain—the decision to make use of the option to adopt batch identification codes.

Moreover, these entities may implement an alternative electronic system for the control and traceability of packaged DOC and IGT wines. Such a system must allow for the unambiguous identification of each container placed on the market through the visible application of a unique, non-serial alphanumeric code or equivalent digital methods, under procedures to be defined by ministerial decree.

The law also entrusts the Minister with the task of issuing a decree to establish the characteristics, markings, and procedures for the manufacture, use, distribution, control, and cost of the seals. The same procedure applies to the definition of the technical characteristics and implementation methods of alternative control and traceability systems.

These seals for wines with a designation of origin have nothing in common with the "fiscal seals" applied to alcoholic beverages, which are intended for excise control and tax payment purposes—except in the case of DOCG and DOC wines in the fortified and/or aromatized categories. In such cases, the application of the fiscal seal pursuant to Ministerial Decree No. 322 of 10 October 2003 is considered to fulfil the legal obligation of seal affixation.

3. Voluntary Use of State Seals for DOC Wines: The Prosecco Model and the Expansion of Traceability Practices"

The voluntary decision to affix a State-issued seal on DOC wines, in order to guarantee the origin of the product and better protect consumers, originated from the ministerial decrees on control plans issued in 2003 and 2007. However, the large-scale dissemination of such seals is chiefly attributable to Decree-Law No. 61 of 8 April 2010 and, more specifically, to the Prosecco DOC Protection Consortium, which, as of 1 August 2011, mandated the use of seals on bottles of Prosecco DOC.

In a 2010 statement issued by the Consortium's President, it was declared: *"The key message to communicate is the concept of traceability and the guarantee for consumers that they are purchasing a product whose production chain—from vineyard to bottle—is subject to full compliance. Prosecco DOC adheres to stringent certification and control rules that guarantee its quality. After securing the legal protection of the name 'Prosecco', it is now necessary to implement all measures to guard against counterfeit 'Made in Italy' products and poor imitations of our Prosecco DOC, which is now State-sealed. This decision reflects the maturity of a region capable of making forward-looking market-oriented choices."*

Following this initiative, many other protection consortia established the mandatory use of seals for DOC wines, including those for Sicilia, Trebbiano and Montepulciano d'Abruzzo, Primitivo di Manduria, Delle Venezie, Verdicchio dei Castelli di Jesi, and Verdicchio di Matelica.

In recent years, there have also been numerous discussions regarding the production of seals for DOCG and DOC wines, particularly in relation to the dismantling of the monopoly held by the Istituto Poligrafico e Zecca dello Stato. This led to the authorization of additional printing houses (*tipografie autorizzate*), allowing for competition in the supply of seals, with the aim of reducing costs and promoting the introduction of alternative traceability systems—especially through the use of alphanumeric coding technologies.

4. Ministerial Decrees Governing the Production and Use of Seals and Alternative Traceability Systems

Among the decrees issued by the Ministry concerning the characteristics, markings, procedures for the manufacture, use, distribution, control, and cost of seals for wines with *Denominazione di Origine Controllata e Garantita* (DOCG) and *Denominazione di Origine Controllata* (DOC), as well as the features and operational modalities of alternative control and traceability systems, the following are to be listed: Decree No. 9374 of 19 April 2011, Decree No. 5888 of 1 March 2012, and Decree No. 2183 of 27 February 2020, which remains in force, although recently amended by Decree of 19 December 2023 (published in the Official Journal on 20 January 2024) and by Decree of 12 March 2025 (published in the Official Journal on 4 April 2025).

With regard to the *"characteristics of the special seal"*, pursuant to the Decree of 27 February 2020, the seal for all wines with a designation of origin is printed by the State Printing Office and Mint (IPZS) using specific security features. The seal certifies the authenticity of the product and incorporates both visible and invisible anti-counterfeiting elements, with traceability managed through dedicated databases.

The seal includes the following indications, printed in a clearly distinguishable color against the background:

10. the emblem of the Italian Republic;
11. the wording “Ministry of Agriculture, Food Sovereignty and Forestry”;
12. the acronym “DOCG” or “DOC”, depending on the classification of the product;
13. a progressive identification number and an alphanumeric series;
14. the nominal volume of the product contained in the packaging, expressed in liters.

5. Introduction of the Italian Tricolour and QR Code in the Updated Seal Layout

With Ministerial Decree of 27 March 2025 (published in Official Journal No. 79 of 4 April 2025), entitled *“Amendment to the Decree of 27 February 2020 concerning the characteristics, markings, procedures for the manufacture, use, distribution, control and cost of seals for wines with Denominazione di Origine Controllata e Garantita (DOCG) and Denominazione di Origine Controllata (DOC), as well as the characteristics and implementation modalities of alternative control and traceability systems”*, the seal layouts were comprehensively revised.

The purpose of the amendment is to update the design of the seals by incorporating the symbol of the Italian national tricolour and by introducing a QR code. Consequently, Annex 1 referred to in Article 3(1) of Ministerial Decree No. 2183 of 27 February 2020 is replaced by a new Annex 1, which also includes the dimensional specifications of the various seal formats.

Annex 1

Ft.o 60,0 x 17,0 mm

Ft.o 80,0 x 17,0 mm

Ft.o 105,0 x 17,0 mm

Ft.o 120,0 x 17,0 mm

Ft.o 60,0 x 17,0 mm

Ft.o 80,0 x 17,0 mm

Ft.o 105,0 x 17,0 mm

Ft.o 120,0 x 17,0 mm

The amendments concern the following elements:

f) the progressive identification number now presented in the form of a QR code (Quick Response Code), which replaces the previous two-dimensional Datamatrix barcode;

f-bis) the inclusion of the Italian tricolour symbol.

In addition to the aforementioned elements, the seal may also include the name of the denomination or the relevant "logo", provided that such indication is foreseen in the corresponding product specification (*disciplinare di produzione*).

6. Operational Requirements for Bottlers: Application, Distribution, and Traceability of Seals"

The other provisions of the Ministerial Decree of 27 February 2020—concerning control bodies, consortia, and operational rules for bottlers—remain unchanged.

With regard to bottlers, the seal must be affixed to the closure system of the containers in such a manner as to prevent any reuse. The information printed on the seal must remain fully legible once affixed to the packaging.

Control bodies, or delegated consortia, are responsible for distributing the seals to bottlers. Seals are collected by entities holding an ICQRF code (for wines bottled in Italy) or by foreign bottlers (for wines bottled abroad). Bottlers are responsible for carrying out the bottling process up to the quantity of certified wine available for sealing, upon presentation of the receipt or payment slip attesting to the payment of the corresponding cost of the seals.

Entities holding the ICQRF code may also collect a quantity of seals corresponding to the volume of wine suitable to become a wine with designation of origin (DO) actually held by the bottler. In such cases, the control body must verify—during inspections and also through the electronic register—the correspondence between the number of seals received and those used or still in stock. Any discrepancies must be reported to the competent ICQRF territorial office.

Bottling companies must record, in dematerialised bottling registers, either the reference to the seals used, the batch identification code, or any alternative traceability system, thereby ensuring full traceability of each lot of DOCG or DOC wine.

For each certified lot of DO wine, a maximum discrepancy of 1.5% is allowed between the number of seals withdrawn and the number of packages actually produced. Should this threshold be objectively and demonstrably exceeded, the bottler must notify the competent ICQRF territorial office and the control body within 24 hours of the occurrence, indicating the cause of deterioration, the quantity of seals affected, and their series and numbering. In the event of seal theft, the bottling company must file a report with the public security authority within 24 hours of the incident and send a copy of the report to both the ICQRF territorial office and the control body.

After conducting the necessary checks, the ICQRF office will authorise the control body to deliver replacement seals for those deteriorated or stolen.

In the event of seal deterioration, bulk sale of the lot, or declassification of a DO wine, the bottler is required to return the corresponding seals to the authorised control body or to the delegated protection consortium.

It is strictly prohibited for bottlers to sell, transfer, or distribute seals within the national territory in connection with sales, transfers, or any other transaction involving bulk lots of DO wines.

Self-adhesive seals must be stored and handled in accordance with the procedures set out in Annex 3 of Ministerial Decree of 27 February 2020.

7. Issuance Costs of State Seals for DOC and DOCG Wines

he ministerial decree sets the unit prices, net of VAT, for State seals affixed to wines with Denominazione di Origine Controllata e Garantita (DOCG) and Denominazione di Origine Controllata (DOC), as follows:

20. **€0.007148** for standard paper-glue State seals for DOC and DOCG wines;

21. **€0.008026** for standard self-adhesive State seals for DOC and DOCG wines.

Personalised paper-glue seals for DOC and DOCG wines:

- a. for single orders of fewer than 100,000,000 units: **€0.009113**;
- b. for single orders of 100,000,000 units or more: **€0.008285**.

Personalised self-adhesive seals for DOC and DOCG wines:

- a. for single orders of fewer than 100,000,000 units: **€0.009971**;
- b. for single orders of 100,000,000 units or more: **€0.009065**.

For both personalised paper-glue and self-adhesive versions, a fixed cost of **€2,974.18** must be added.

Personalised seals with full-colour logo for DOC and DOCG wines, paper-glue version:

- a. for single orders of fewer than 100,000,000 units: **€0.009988**;
- b. for single orders of 100,000,000 units or more: **€0.009648**.

Personalised seals with full-colour logo for DOC and DOCG wines, self-adhesive version:

- a. for single orders of fewer than 100,000,000 units: **€0.010846**;
- b. for single orders of 100,000,000 units or more: **€0.010476**.

For both the paper-glue and self-adhesive versions with coloured logo, a fixed cost of **€4,899.40** is to be added.

These prices apply to the transfer of seals from the *Istituto Poligrafico e Zecca dello Stato S.p.A.* to the control bodies or delegated consortia. For the final price charged to bottling companies, additional costs must be included for transportation, management, and distribution services of the seals, as incurred by the control bodies or their designated consortia. These costs must be reimbursed by the bottling companies, proportionally to the actual cost of the service rendered.

8. Provisions on Alternative Control and Traceability Systems

Article 10 of the Ministerial Decree of 27 February 2020, adopted pursuant to Article 48(8) of Law No. 238/2016, established a telematic system of control and traceability for packaged PDO and PGI wines as an alternative to the use of certification strips (fascette). Under this system, each container of PDO or PGI wine placed on the market had to bear a unique non-serial alphanumeric code, clearly affixed, enabling the competent control authorities to identify the individual container.

The code was required to:

- be visibly affixed to each individual container during the bottling and labelling process, at the same facility;
- be fully legible, once affixed to the container, without requiring decoding or reading devices;
- allow for the unique identification of the company (hereinafter referred to as the "provider") that generated and supplied it;
- be associated, prior to the placing on the market of the container, with all data relating to the bottled wine product as specified in the request submitted to the control body.

However, these provisions were repealed and amended by the Ministerial Decree of 19 December 2023, which states:

"*Considering the high level of competence, experience, and professionalism of the Italian State Printing Office and Mint (IPZS), in particular in the printing and issuance of certification strips for DOCG and DOC wines, as established by the Ministerial Decree of the Ministry of Economy and Finance of 23 December 2013 identifying value documents pursuant to Article 2(10-bis), letters a) and b) of Law No. 559 of 13 July 1966 and subsequent amendments, Annex A, No. 13. It is therefore deemed necessary, in the interest of more effective traceability and anti-counterfeiting safeguards, and for administrative efficiency and simplification, to amend Article 10 of the aforementioned Ministerial Decree No. 2183 of 27 February 2020.*"

Specifically, the Ministerial Decree of 19 December 2023 modifies Article 10 of Decree No. 2183/2020 by deleting letter c) of paragraph 2 ("allow for the unique identification of the company (hereinafter referred to as the 'provider') that generated and supplied it") and replacing paragraph 3 as follows:

> "*The telematic control and traceability system is provided by the IPZS. It is equipped with anti-counterfeiting systems and traceability managed through dedicated databases. The value documents (contrassegni) for the telematic system, as an alternative to the use of certification strips, in addition to the non-serial alphanumeric code referred to in paragraph 2, shall also bear a two-dimensional barcode for automated reading and shall conform in format, dimensions, and*

features to those indicated in Annex 4, which constitutes an integral part of this decree."

Paragraph 5 is also amended to state:

> *"The responsibility for requesting from the IPZS the management and distribution of the contrassegni referred to in paragraph 3 lies with the control bodies or with the consortia delegated by them, according to the agreements set forth in a specific convention. The control plan must provide evidence of such a convention."*

Some trade associations have expressed concerns regarding these amendments to the Decree of 27 February 2020. These include potential confusion among consumers (particularly between IG and DO wines) and possible incompatibility with the Consolidated Wine Law, especially with respect to the decision not to open the market for the printing of such identifiers, instead entrusting it entirely to the IPZS.

Additionally, the Ministerial Decree of 19 December 2023 introduces Article 10-bis on the **Costs for Issuing Traceability Contrassegni**, which sets the maximum unit prices, excluding VAT, for contrassegni used in the telematic system for DOC and IGT wines as follows:

- €0.0045 for standard version contrassegni (paper with glue);
- €0.0055 for standard version contrassegni (self-adhesive paper).

Annex 4 of the decree provides the template models for the contrassegni to be used for IGT wines.

The first Consortium to request State-issued contrassegni (identification strips) for wines with Protected Geographical Indication (Indicazione Geografica Tipica – IGT) was the *Sannio Consorzio Tutela Vini*, for the IGT *Benevento*, effective from 1 August 2024. This marks the beginning of the new system that includes a "digital passport" accessible via a QR code. According to the Consortium's statement:

> *"This is a historic initiative for the Italian wine sector, as until now, State-issued contrassegni were reserved exclusively for DOCG and DOC wines. The introduction of State identifiers for wines with geographical indications offers the wine supply chain a competitive advantage in terms of authenticity, brand protection, and marketing, while enhancing consumer trust, traceability, and legal protection of products."*

Similarly, the *Consorzio Tutela Vini Emilia* has announced the implementation of anti-counterfeiting contrassegni starting from 1 August 2025. This Consortium represents one of the most significant IGT denominations in terms of volume, with over 120 million bottles produced annually—90% of which are classified as *Lambrusco IGT*. The new contrassegno will feature a QR code scannable by consumers, giving access to a *Digital Wine Passport*. This section will provide key data, including the serial and control code of the seal, the production year, the batch number, and the certification details. Additional information will be available on the producer, the relevant protection consortium, and the certifying body, along with suggested food pairings and recipes that enhance the value of Emilia IGT wines.

It remains to be seen whether other protection consortia will follow this path by choosing to introduce State-issued contrassegni for IGT wines as well.

The European Geographical Indications Reform Is Nearing Completion

By Giordano Zinzani, oenologist and expert in wine legislation

Summary: **1. The New European Regulatory Framework for Geographical Indications: Structure and Entry into Force - 2. Implementing Regulation (EU) 2025/26 - 3. Delegated Regulation (EU) 2025/27 - 4. Delegated Regulation (EU) 2025/28 - 5. Delegated Regulation (EU) 2025/29 - 6. Implementation of the Geographical Indications Reform at the National Level - 7. EUIPO – Conference on Geographical Indications**

1. The New European Regulatory Framework for Geographical Indications: Structure and Entry into Force

The Official Journal of the European Union of April 23, 2024, published Regulation (EU) 2024/1143 of the European Parliament and of the Council of April 11, 2024, "on geographical indications (GIs) for wines, spirit drinks, and agricultural products, as well as on traditional specialities guaranteed (TSG) and optional quality terms for agricultural products, amending Regulations (EU) No. 1308/2013, (EU) 2019/787, and (EU) 2019/1753, and repealing Regulation (EU) No. 1151/2012." The new Regulation has entered into force, in part, as of May 13, 2024; however, for some articles, application was set to begin on January 1, 2025.

The Regulation sets out the rules concerning the quality schemes:
a) protected designations of origin and protected geographical indications for wines; protected designations of origin and protected geographical indications for agricultural products, including foodstuffs; and geographical indications for spirit drinks;
b) traditional specialities guaranteed and optional quality terms for agricultural products, including foodstuffs.

Regulation 2024/1143 represents a significant milestone: it brings together all agri-food, wine, and spirit drink products with Geographical Indication under a single legislative basis, strengthens the role of Consortia for protection, and provides more effective tools for the competitive and sustainable development of quality production. The objectives are to strengthen the legislative framework of the "Geographical Indications System," improve sustainable integration into the European quality policy, and reinforce the position of GI producers in the food supply chain.

With this Regulation, stricter protections for Geographical Indications (GIs) come into force, including a ban on registering traditional terms identical to or reminiscent of PDO or PGI names; it will be mandatory to indicate the producer's name on the label of a Protected Designation of Origin (PDO) or Protected Geographical Indication (PGI), in order to ensure maximum transparency for consumers. The regulation also includes measures to protect Geographical Indications online and gives producers greater powers by streamlining the GI registration process.

To complete the legislative framework at the EU level, implementing and delegated acts were still required; these were published in the Official Journal of the European Union on January 15, 2025, and entered into force on January 18. These are four Regulations:

15. **Implementing Regulation (EU) 2025/26** on registrations, amendments, cancellations, enforcement of protection, labelling, and communication concerning GIs and TSGs, amending Implementing Regulation (EU) 2019/34 regarding GIs in the wine sector and repealing Implementing Regulations (EU) No. 668/2014 and (EU) 2021/1236;
16. **Delegated Regulation (EU) 2025/27** on the registration and protection of GIs, TSGs, and optional quality terms, repealing Delegated Regulation (EU) No. 664/2014;
17. **Delegated Regulation (EU) 2025/28,** amending Delegated Regulation (EU) 2019/33, supplementing Regulation (EU) No. 1308/201 for applications for protection of designations of origin, geographical indications, and traditional terms in the wine sector, the opposition procedure, use restrictions, amendment of product specifications, cancellation of protection, as well as labelling and presentation;
18. **Delegated Regulation (EU) 2025/29,** repealing Delegated Regulation (EU) 2021/1235, which supplemented Regulation (EU) 2019/787 with rules on GI applications for spirit drinks, amendments to product specifications, cancellation of registration, and the register.

2. Implementing Regulation (EU) 2025/26

The implementing regulation lays down the rules for the application of Regulation (EU) 2024/1143 with regard to:

a) the procedures for applications for registration, approval of Union amendments, notification of ordinary amendments, cancellation of registrations, management of the Union register of geographical indications, and the establishment of a system for certifying compliance with the specifications for geographical indications;
b) the procedures for applications for registration, approval of amendments, cancellation of registrations, management of the Union register of traditional specialities guaranteed, and the establishment of a system for certifying compliance with the specifications for traditional specialities guaranteed;
c) the labelling and communication requirements concerning geographical indications and traditional specialities guaranteed.

Applications for registration must include: the "single document," supporting documentation, the Member State's declaration certifying that the application meets the requirements for registration, any transitional period granted or proposed by national authorities following the national examination and opposition procedure, information on any admissible opposition, and a reference to the electronic publication of the updated specification, all using the forms provided in the Commission's digital system.
The single document for GIs of agricultural products and spirit drinks must be concise and must not exceed 2,500 words. For wine GIs, the limit is 5,000 words. The single document indicates the classification of the product by reference to the heading and code of the Combined Nomenclature. It may include requirements relating to packaging and labelling or other applicable requirements as provided in the specification. The geographical area must be defined clearly and precisely, referring, wherever possible, to physical or administrative boundaries. Maps may be attached to the application. Applications for the registration of a name or an amendment may contain the description of two or more distinct products authorized to use the GI in question.

The regulation provides, in various articles, rules concerning amendments to the specification during the application procedure, submission of oppositions and notifications of consultation outcomes, and communications relating to the approval of ordinary or temporary amendments.

A register of Union geographical indications is established as a digital solution that enables the technical storage and public access to all entries relating to geographical indications, including applications for registration, Union amendments and cancellation requests, rejections, publications for opposition purposes, registrations, approvals of Union amendments, publications of ordinary and temporary amendments, and cancellations. The Commission is the owner of this Union register. The digital solution is managed by the European Union Intellectual Property Office (EUIPO), which hosts it on its servers, and it is available in all the official languages of the Union.

With regard to "proof of origin," the specification of a PDO or PGI must set out the procedures that operators must put in place to provide the relevant elements concerning proof of origin for the product, raw materials, animal feed, and any other elements that, according to the specification, must originate from the defined geographical area.

A chapter of Implementing Regulation 2025/26 is dedicated, similarly to geographical indications, to the rules for traditional specialities guaranteed, as provided for in Regulation (EU) 2024/1143. It should be recalled that the traditional specialities guaranteed (TSG) scheme was established (excluding the wine sector) to safeguard traditional production methods and recipes by:
a) helping producers of traditional products to market their goods and communicate to consumers the characteristics that add value to their traditional recipes and products;
b) fostering value creation by contributing to fair competition in the supply chain, ensuring fair income for producers, and supporting the objectives of rural development policy.

The registration and protection of traditional specialities guaranteed does not relieve producers of the obligation to comply with other Union provisions, particularly those concerning product marketing, the single Common Market Organisation, and food labelling.

The Regulation includes several "Annexes" specifying the required format for "single documents," applications, specifications, attestations, and various communications.

For the labelling of PGI, PDO, and TSG products, the use of "Union symbols" is provided for, which must be reproduced in accordance with Annex XVII of the Regulation. The Union symbols, their indications, or the corresponding abbreviations, if shown on the product label, must be accompanied by the registered name. The terms "PROTECTED DESIGNATION OF ORIGIN",

“PROTECTED GEOGRAPHICAL INDICATION”, and “TRADITIONAL SPECIALITY GUARANTEED” within the symbol may be used in any of the official languages of the Union.
For Union symbols, if colours are used, direct colours (Pantone) or four-colour process printing may be employed.

Union symbols in Pantone:

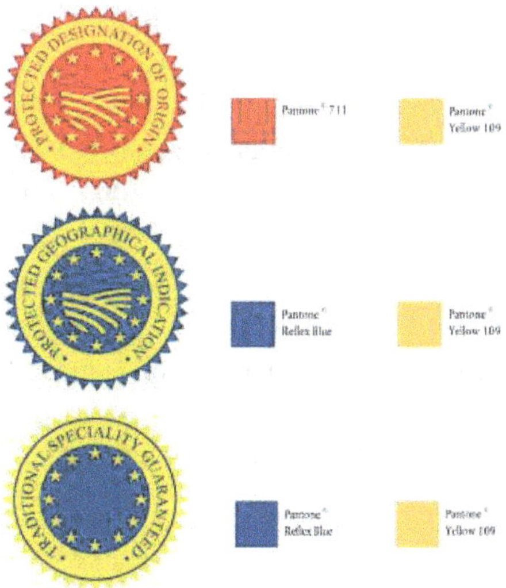

For four-colour process printing, the following colour mixes are indicated:

- **Yellow: 10% magenta – 90% yellow**
- **Blue: 100% cyan – 80% magenta**
- **Red: 100% magenta – 80% yellow**

If the symbol is not clearly visible due to the colour used in the symbol itself or its background, an external border can be drawn around the symbol to make it stand out more distinctly against the background.

The use of black and white versions of the symbols is permitted only if black and white are the sole colours used on the packaging, and the regulation provides specific examples in this regard.

For printing purposes, uppercase Times Roman font must be used for the text. The minimum size of the Union symbols is 15 mm in diameter; however, for packaging or products of small dimensions, the diameter may be reduced to 10 mm.
The same regulation also lists, in all official languages of the Union, the possible translations and abbreviations of:

"Protected Designation of Origin"

"Protected Geographical Indication"

"Traditional Speciality Guaranteed"

3. Delegated Regulation (EU) 2025/27

Delegated Regulation (EU) 2025/27, which repeals Regulation No. 664/2014, consists of 14 articles and also entered into force on 18 January. This regulation supplements Regulation (EU) 2024/1143 with regard to the following aspects:

a) As regards geographical indications:

i) procedural rules concerning oppositions;

ii) procedures for Union amendments;

iii) the approval and notification of standard amendments, including temporary amendments;
iv) the relationship between Union amendments and standard amendments;

v) requirements concerning the origin of raw materials for geographical indications of agricultural products;

b) As regards traditional specialities guaranteed:

i) procedures for registration applications;

ii) procedural rules concerning oppositions;

iii) procedures for the approval of amendments to the product specification;

iv) rules governing the use of traditional specialities guaranteed that designate a product used as an ingredient in the name of a processed product.

The product specification for traditional specialities guaranteed is subject to length limitations: it must be concise and not exceed 5,000 words. An application for the approval of a modification to the specification must also be concise and must not exceed 7,500 words, including the specification itself.

Article 12 of this regulation governs the use of traditional specialities guaranteed that designate a product used as an ingredient in the name of a processed product.

4. Delegated Regulation (EU) 2025/28

Delegated Regulation (EU) 2025/28 consists of only two articles. This regulation modifies the title of Delegated Regulation (EU) 2019/33, which is replaced with the following:

"Commission Delegated Regulation (EU) 2019/33 of 17 October 2018 supplementing Regulation (EU) No 1308/2013 of the European Parliament and of the Council as regards applications for protection and the labelling of designations of origin and geographical indications, applications for protection, the opposition procedure, the amendment and cancellation of traditional terms, as well as labelling and presentation in the wine sector."

Article 1 of Regulation 2019/33 is also amended and now reads as follows:

Article 1 – Subject matter

This Regulation lays down supplementary rules to Regulation (EU) No 1308/2013:

a) with regard to protected designations of origin and protected geographical indications in the wine sector:

(i) the name to be protected;

(ii) additional requirements for product specifications;

(iii) derogations concerning production within the defined geographical area;

(iv) derogations from the obligation to use the “indications” on labels;

b) with regard to traditional terms in the wine sector:

(i) applications for protection;

(ii) the opposition procedure;

(iii) amendments;

(iv) cancellation;

c) with regard to the wine sector in general: labelling and presentation.

The following provisions are repealed: Article 2(2), Article 3, Article 4(1), and Articles 7 to 21.

Article 59 is amended regarding the language of documents: they must be drafted in one of the official languages of the Union.

5. Delegated Regulation (EU) 2025/29

Delegated Regulation (EU) 2025/29 repeals Delegated Regulation (EU) 2021/1235, which had supplemented Regulation (EU) 2019/787, but whose provisions are now outdated and replaced by the newly adopted regulations described above.

6. Implementation of the Geographical Indications Reform at the National Level

Now that the European regulatory framework has been defined with the publication of the implementing and delegated acts, national implementing measures are required to align domestic provisions with the practical application of the "Geographical Indications Reform," which also includes the wine sector under a unified European text. This long-awaited reform, in force since May 2024 as outlined above, strengthens the role of protection consortia, enhances international protection for geographical indications, clarifies the production rules applicable to PGI wines, and simplifies the procedures related to product specifications.

Currently, the national legislative instrument in force governing the procedures for submitting and examining applications for the protection of PDOs, PGIs, traditional terms for wine products, applications for amendments to product specifications and traditional terms, and for cancellation of protection, is the Ministerial Decree of 6 December 2021.

7. EUIPO – Conference on Geographical Indications

On 28 and 29 January, the EUIPO hosted a conference on Geographical Indications titled *"Safeguarding Our Heritage, Cultivating Our Future"*, held in Alicante. The two-day event focused on the upcoming changes following the introduction of new rules concerning the protection of GIs for craft and industrial products, as well as agricultural GIs, aiming to improve protection and simplify the registration process. The conference was opened by João Negrão, Executive Director of the EUIPO, the agency now responsible for the management of GIs for craft and industrial products. Among the various speakers was also the European Commissioner for Agriculture, Christophe Hansen, who highlighted the crucial role of GIs in promoting sustainability and innovation, as well as the importance of ensuring a robust mechanism to safeguard the added value of European GIs.

Amendments to the Regulation on Oenological Practices and the Production of Organic Dealcoholized Wines

By Giordano Zinzani, oenologist and expert in wine legislation

The authorised oenological practices and the applicable restrictions on the production and preservation of wine products are governed by Delegated Regulation (EU) 2019/934, which supplements Regulation (EU) No. 1308/2013. Since its entry into force in June 2019, this regulation has already undergone several amendments. Most recently, further modifications—taking into account technical progress and, in particular, the resolutions adopted by the OIV in 2022 and 2023—have been introduced by Delegated Regulation 2024/3085 of 30 September 2024, published in the Official Journal of the EU on 9 December 2024 (amending Delegated Regulation (EU) 2019/934 with regard to authorised oenological practices), which entered into force on 29 December 2024.

Regulation 2024/3085 has amended Annex I, thereby revising Table 1 – Authorised Oenological Practices and Table 2 – Authorised Oenological Compounds. Furthermore, the amendments also concern Annex III of Regulation (EU) 2019/934, which includes lists or characteristics of specific wines—though not referring to Italian products in this case. The amended points cover a range of issues relating to practices and authorised

oenological compounds. A summary of the changes introduced follows below:

In Table 1, under entries 2 and 2 bis, explanatory footnotes have been added to better clarify the scope of "thermal treatments" and "cold treatments" by listing the general categories of processes concerned.

1. Thermal treatments

Thermal treatments include:

19. maceration following grape heating,
20. pasteurization,
21. interruption of alcoholic fermentation by heat,
22. post-fermentative hot maceration,
23. and hot bottling.

Cold treatments include:

22. pre-fermentative cold maceration,
23. cryoconcentration,
24. interruption of alcoholic fermentation by cold,
25. cold-induced deacidification,
26. and cold stabilization.

2. Flotation

Regarding flotation, the permitted conditions and limits of use now state: *"Only when using nitrogen, argon, or aeration."* The reference to the use of carbon dioxide has been removed, while the reference to argon has been added.

3. Oenological Practices Requiring Supervision

The implementation of certain oenological practices or the use of specific oenological compounds must be supervised by an oenologist or a qualified or specialized technician, due to their important role in ensuring both operator safety and the safety and quality of the final product. To clarify which practices require such supervision, several entries in Tables 1 and 2 have been amended.

Table 1 – Oenological Practices Requiring Supervision

- 6 – Ion exchange resins
- 10 – Electrodialysis treatment
- 12 – Adjustment of wine alcohol content
- 13 – Cation exchangers for tartaric stabilization
- 14 – Electromembrane treatment
- 15 – Cation exchangers for acidification
- 16 – Coupled membrane processes
- 17 – Membrane contactors
- 18 – Wine treatment using membrane technology combined with adsorption on activated carbon or styrene-divinylbenzene adsorbent beads
- 20 – Partial concentration

Table 2 – Authorized Oenological Compounds Requiring Supervision

- 6.5 – Potassium ferrocyanide
- 6.6 – Calcium phytate
- 6.9 – D, L-tartaric acid or its neutral potassium salt
- 6.12 – Polyvinylimidazole–polyvinylpyrrolidone copolymers (PVI/PVP)

4. Treatment of Wine Using Membrane Technology Combined with Adsorption on Activated Carbon or Styrene-Divinylbenzene Adsorbent Beads

o reduce excessive concentrations of volatile phenols—specifically 4-ethylphenol and 4-ethylguaiacol—wine treatment using membrane technology combined with activated carbon had already been permitted. In 2023, the OIV adopted a resolution expanding the scope of this treatment to allow the use of styrene-divinylbenzene adsorbent beads in addition to activated carbon, thereby covering all volatile phenols. This amendment enables wine producers to further correct organoleptic defects in wine. The membranes used must comply with the requirements of Regulation (EC) No 1935/2004 and Regulation (EU) No 10/2011, as well as any applicable national implementing provisions.

5. Purity Requirements and Specifications for Substances Used in Oenological Practices

Article 9(1) of Delegated Regulation (EU) 2019/934 stipulates that the purity requirements and specifications for substances used in oenological practices are those established under Commission Regulation (EU) No 231/2012. If not listed in that regulation, the specifications set by the OIV International Code of Oenological Practices apply. Previously, Column 4 of Table 2 referenced the relevant OIV Code sheets for all substances listed in the table, including those already governed by Regulation (EU) No 231/2012—creating potential confusion. To clarify, the reference to the OIV Code sheet has now been deleted for those substances whose specifications are governed by Regulation (EU) No 231/2012.

6. Ascorbic Acid

Ascorbic acid occurs naturally in grapes, must, and wine, and may also be added in the form of L-ascorbic acid (E300) as a preservative and antioxidant. The OIV has established that up to 300 mg/L of ascorbic acid may be present in wine placed on the market. Therefore, the regulation now removes the previously existing maximum limit of 250 mg/L per individual treatment, as long as the total ascorbic acid content in the marketed wine does not exceed 300 mg/L.

7. Use of Selective Vegetable Fibres

Among the authorized oenological compounds classified as "adsorbents," selective vegetable fibres were previously permitted for use in wine. This authorization is now extended to include musts as well.

8. Requirements and Specifications for Microcrystalline Cellulose

The requirements and specifications for microcrystalline cellulose used as an activator in alcoholic and malolactic fermentation must comply with those set out in the annex to Regulation (EU) No 231/2012. The previously stated conditions of use were redundant with Article 9(1) of Delegated Regulation (EU) 2019/934, and have therefore been removed.

9. Diammonium Hydrogen Phosphate

For diammonium hydrogen phosphate used as a fermentation activator, Table 2 mistakenly included the E number E 342. Since this additive does not correspond to any E number within EU legislation, the reference was removed.

10. Powdered Cellulose

Given that powdered cellulose (E 460) and food-grade cellulose used as a fermentation activator for alcoholic and malolactic fermentation are the same substance, Table 2, item 4.10, now lists only "Powdered Cellulose."

11. Tannins

The specific monographs for tannins are currently under revision by the OIV. Pending the outcome of this revision, only the relevant sections of the oenological code sheets have been cited under the applicable conditions and usage limits.

12. Gum Arabic

Gum Arabic is used as a stabilizing agent. The maximum allowable dose for its use in wine had already been published in the document titled "List and Description of the OIV Oenological Code Sheets Referred to in Article 3(2) of Commission Delegated Regulation (EU) 2019/934" (Official Journal of the EU, 6 May 2022): the permitted dose must not exceed 0.3 g/L.

3.3.6. TREATMENT WITH GUM ARABIC (12/72)

Requirements:

a) the product must be added to the wine after final filtration or immediately prior to bottling;
b) the dose used must not exceed 0.3 g/L;

c) gum arabic must comply with the specifications of the OIV International Code of Oenological Practices.

However, in light of findings by the OIV indicating that a dose of 0.3 g/L is insufficient to stabilize colloidal color substances in some highly pigmented fortified red wines, and that a higher dose of 0.8 g/L is necessary to achieve stabilization without affecting the wine's organoleptic properties, the prescription has been amended. With Resolution OIV-OENO 689-2022, the regulation now reads:

"The dose of use shall not exceed 0.8 g/L for fortified red wines and 0.3 g/L for other wines." (equivalent to 30 grams per hectolitre).

This amendment has been incorporated into Table 2 of Regulation (EU) 2019/934. News of the revision, especially the limit of 0.3 g/L for wines other than fortified reds, has sparked controversy in France, where some producers customarily use higher doses, particularly for red wines.

13. Enzymes

Regarding the conditions and limits of use for the eleven authorized enzymes, the previous specifications have generally been removed to align directly with the OIV's provisions.

At present, the only enzyme with hemicellulase activity authorized by the OIV is xylanase. Consequently, Table 2 has been updated with the correct reference to xylanase.

The OIV's International Code of Oenological Practices permits the use of β-glucanase (β1-3, β1-6) in both musts and wines for clarification, filtration, and solubilization of yeast-derived compounds. In order to harmonize EU regulations with the OIV's recommendations, the corresponding OIV sheets have been added and the list of eligible wine product categories has been revised accordingly.

The reference to glycosidase has been removed from the list of approved enzymes.

14. Caramel

Among the "other practices," the regulation authorizes the use of caramel in the production of fortified wines, previously listed under the general name "caramel." However, under Regulation (EC) No 1333/2008 on food additives, each version of E 150 has a specific designation:

- E 150a = plain caramel
- E 150b = caustic sulfite caramel
- E 150c = ammonium caramel
- E 150d = sulfite ammonium caramel

Accordingly, four separate entries have been established for E 150a, E 150b, E 150c, and E 150d, as designated by Regulation (EC) No 1333/2008.

15. Authorized Oenological Practices and Restrictions for Fortified Wines and Fortified Wines with PDO or PGI

Regulation 2024/3085 also introduced amendments to Annex III of Regulation (EU) 2019/934, which sets forth the authorized oenological practices and specific restrictions applicable to fortified wines and those with PDO or PGI.

In particular:

- French white PDO wines "Corrèze" bearing the traditional term "Vin de paille" possess a high residual sugar content and have been authorized to use sulfur dioxide up to 300 mg/L for preservation purposes.
- Fortified wines undergoing extended aging may now have a minimum actual alcoholic strength of 14% vol (instead of the previously required 15% vol). Spain requested the inclusion of several Spanish fortified wines in this revised list.
- Fortified wines must generally have a total alcoholic strength of no less than 17.5% vol unless a derogation applies. Relevant amendments to these provisions have been made.
- Changes were also introduced concerning the traditional terms "vino generoso" and "vino generoso de licor."
- Updates were made to the list of Spanish PDO wines and the provisions relating to the Portuguese PDO "Porto."

16. Amendment to the Organic Production Regulation: Dealcoholised Wine

While in Italy there are still doubts surrounding the production of dealcoholised or partially dealcoholised wine, the European Union has already opened the door to the production of organic dealcoholised wine. Given that dealcoholisation cannot be achieved through traditional organic methods, a request—primarily from German producers—was made to amend the regulation governing the production of organic dealcoholised wine. This amendment was adopted with **Commission Delegated Regulation (EU) 2025/405 of 13 December 2024**, published in the **Official Journal of the EU on 26 February 2025**, which **amends Regulation (EU) 2018/848 of the European Parliament and of the Council as regards oenological practices**.

It should be recalled that **Regulation (EU) 2018/848** governs **organic production and labelling of organic products**. Following **Regulation (EU) 2021/2117**, dealcoholised wine was officially included among the products of the wine sector, and a new section on dealcoholisation processes was introduced in the list of authorised oenological practices. Consequently, the **specific production rules for the wine sector** listed in **Annex II, Part VI of Regulation (EU) 2018/848** have been amended.

The amendment inserts the following under **point 3.3 of Annex II, Part VI - Wine** of Regulation (EU) 2018/848:

(c) Partial vacuum evaporation, pursuant to Annex VIII, Part I, Section E, point (a) of Regulation (EU) No 1308/2013, either alone or in combination with the distillation referred to in point (d) of this section, provided that partial vacuum evaporation is used solely for the production of dealcoholised wine with an actual alcoholic strength by volume not exceeding **0.5% vol**, that the operating temperature does not exceed **75°C**, and that the filtration pore size is not smaller than **0.2 micrometres**;

(d) Distillation, pursuant to Annex VIII, Part I, Section E, point (c) of Regulation (EU) No 1308/2013, either alone or in combination with the partial vacuum evaporation referred to in point (c), provided that distillation is used solely for the production of dealcoholised wine with an actual alcoholic strength by volume not exceeding **0.5% vol**, that it is carried out under vacuum, that the temperature does not exceed **75°C**, and that the filtration pore size is not smaller than **0.2 micrometres**.

As a result of these amendments, from **18 March 2025**—the date of entry into force of the regulation—**vacuum evaporation and/or distillation** will become **authorised oenological practices** in the production of **organic dealcoholised wine** in the EU. These techniques, however, are allowed **only** for wines that are **fully dealcoholised** (alcohol content not exceeding 0.5% vol), and **not** for **partially dealcoholised wines**.

Highlights from the 2024 OIV General Assembly and New Resolutions for the Wine Sector

By Giordano Zinzani, oenologist and expert in wine legislation

Summary: **1. OIV 2024 General Assembly and Strategic Outlook: Highlights from the 45th World Congress of Vine and Wine - 2. OIV Recommendations on the Application of Agroecological Principles in the Vitivinicultural Sector – OIV-VITI 680-2024 - 3. OIV Definitions and Recommendations on Old Vines and Old Vineyards in the Vitivinicultural Sector – OIV-VITI 703-2024 - 4. OIV Definition and Recommendations on the Importance of Mountain and Steep Slope Viticulture for the Vitivinicultural Sector – OIV-VITI 716-2024 - 5. Use of Fumaric Acid for Wine Acidification – OIV-OENO 581B-2024 - 6. Treatment with Functionalised Mesoporous Silica (FMS) for Protein Stabilisation of Wines – OIV-OENO 672B-2024 - 7. Update to the Monograph and Codex on**

Plant Protein Substances (Removal of Wheat) – OIV-OENO 723-2024 - 8. Update to the Monographs on Primary and Secondary Products of Non-Saccharomyces Yeasts – OIV-OENO 740-202 - 9. Analytical Parameters Commonly Used for Wines and Sparkling Wines – OIV-OENO 712A-2024 - 10. Determination of Mineral Elements in Grape Juice, Reconstituted Grape Juice, Concentrated Grape Juice, and Grape Nectar – OIV-OENO 662K-2024 - 11. Update to the International Standard for Wine Labelling: Grape Variety Name – OIV-ECO 696-2024 - 12. Update to the OIV International Standard for Wine Labelling – Electronic Label, Nutritional Declaration, and Ingredient Indication – OIV-ECO 676-2024 - 13. Revised OIV Regulation on International Competitions for Wines and Wine-Based Spirits – OIV-OENO 671C-2024 - 14. Repeal of Obsolete, Outdated and Redundant OIV Resolutions – OIV-ECO 726-2024

1. OIV 2024 General Assembly and Strategic Outlook: Highlights from the 45th World Congress of Vine and Wine

The OIV General Assembly in Dijon, France, marked the conclusion of the 45th World Congress of Vine and Wine, held from 14 to 18 October 2024. The Congress was organized to coincide with the Centenary of the OIV and gathered 756 participants from over 40 countries. The event featured scientific presentations, digital posters, and printed posters displayed on-site.

The International Organisation of Vine and Wine (OIV) is the global scientific and technical reference body for the wine sector. It is an intergovernmental organization, composed of member States. With the recent accession of China (the third-largest country in terms of vineyard surface area), the number of OIV member States has reached 51, thereby increasing the Organization's representativeness to 85% of the world's vineyard area.

During the General Assembly, South African economist and information technology expert Yvette van der Merwe was elected as the new President of the OIV for a three-year term, succeeding Italian Professor Luigi Moio, who was appointed Vice-President. Van der Merwe has dedicated her 30-year career to the South African wine industry and was already serving within the OIV as Chair of the "Economy and Law" Commission.

The newly elected Chairs of the OIV Commissions and Sub-Commissions are as follows:

24. Commission I “Viticulture”: Mario de la Fuente (Spain)

25. Commission II “Oenology”: Valérie Lempereur (France)

26. Commission III “Economy and Law”: Alberto Ribeiro de Almeida (Portugal)

27. Commission IV “Safety and Health”: Angelika Paschke-Kratzin (Germany)

28. Sub-Commission “Methods of Analysis”: Fernanda Spinelli (Brazil)

29. Sub-Commission “Table Grapes, Dried Grapes and Non-Fermented Vine Products”: Rodrigo Sebastián Espíndola (Argentina)

During the Assembly, the new Strategic Plan of the OIV for 2025–2029 was also adopted, structured around six priorities aimed at addressing global challenges in the vitivinicultural sector:

27. Coordinate approaches to sustainability

28. Promote resilient and sustainable viticulture

29. Adapt oenology to future needs

30. Support all wine products

31. Simplify international trade

32. Contribute to consumer safety and provide in-depth information on vine, wine, and society

On 29 November 2024, the date marking the 100th anniversary of the signing of the OIV's founding treaty, the Director General of the Organization, John Barker, presented preliminary findings from a study examining the vine and wine sector over the past century. The analysis covered data from 79 wine-producing countries. On the same occasion, the head of the OIV Statistics Department also presented the first estimates of wine production for 2024. Due to the impact of climate change, a decline is forecasted: -2% compared to 2023, and -13% compared to the ten-year average. Global wine production for the 2024 harvest is estimated between 227 and 235 million hectolitres.

Returning to the OIV Congress and General Assembly, a key moment was the approval of official decisions — the “Resolutions.” Thirteen in total, these covered topics such as agroecology, viticulture, oenology, winemaking practices, safety, labelling, analytics, and more. As agreed with the EU, the resolutions on oenological practices will lead to updates of the relevant Regulation, and analytical methods will become "official methods." On this matter, Regulation (EU) 2024/3085, amending Commission Regulation (EU) 2019/934 and integrating Regulation (EU) No 1308/2013 on authorized oenological practices, was recently published in the Official Journal of the EU on 9 December 2024. This amendment was necessary to reflect technical advances, particularly the OIV resolutions adopted in 2022 and 2023, and to expand, among other things, the list of fortified wines eligible for derogations on minimum actual alcoholic strength.

The full texts of the "2024 Resolutions" adopted span more than forty pages. This work highlights the most relevant points, referring the reader to the official OIV documentation for further detail.

2. OIV Recommendations on the Application of Agroecological Principles in the Vitivinicultural Sector – OIV-VITI 680-2024

Following proposals submitted by Commission I "Viticulture" and the Expert Group on "Sustainable Development and Climate Change," and taking into account previous resolutions, as well as the positions adopted by the FAO and the United Nations Convention on Biological Diversity, the OIV has adopted the following agroecological principles applicable to the vitivinicultural sector:

- Safeguarding human, social, and cultural values that support food culture and traditions, while fostering solidarity-based economies.
- Supporting cultural values and food traditions linked to vitiviniculture, which play a social role in shaping cultural identity and a sense of belonging to territories and food systems.
- Promoting the development of solidarity-based economies that foster local economic growth and strengthen the social foundations for inclusive and sustainable development.
- Fostering co-creation and exchange of agroecological knowledge in the sector, in order to promote responsible governance at all levels among stakeholders.
- Adapting the economic profitability of enterprises by integrating environmental, social, and governance (ESG) principles into management strategies and core values.
- Enhancing farm autonomy by reducing the use of fertilizers, plant protection products, water, and fossil fuels.

- Adopting a regenerative approach through the use of cover crops, crop associations, minimal soil tillage, compost, and a reduced reliance on chemical pesticides and fertilizers.
- Strengthening vineyard protection by improving the ecological health of vitivinicultural agroecosystems, enhancing overall biodiversity, and promoting soil health as a strategy for adapting to climate change. This goal is to be achieved through:

  a) vineyard management that prioritizes preventive measures, including prophylaxis, exploitation of varietal resistance or tolerance, improvement of soil quality and health, biodiversity enhancement through habitat management, and, where possible, diversification of land use to reduce the agroecosystem's susceptibility to biotic stressors;

  b) integration of traditional physical, biological, and genetic techniques with recent technological innovations in crop protection, such as biocontrol products and decision-support tools that also enhance energy efficiency.

The OIV encourages its Member States to consider vitivinicultural agroecology as one of the many innovative approaches to sustainable viticulture.

3. OIV Definitions and Recommendations on Old Vines and Old Vineyards in the Vitivinicultural Sector – OIV-VITI 703-2024

As a result of the work carried out by the Commission on "Viticulture" and the Expert Group on "Genetic Resources and Grapevine Selection," and in order to promote environmentally respectful viticulture, safeguard natural resources and biodiversity, and foster sustainable development and the preservation of the heritage embodied by grapevine varieties, the OIV acknowledges that the evolution of a plant's phenotypic expression over time is the result of:

- The techniques used for its propagation and planting (own-rooted vine, field grafted or bench grafted);
- The varieties and genotypes employed as scions and rootstocks, and their respective genotypic traits;
- The cumulative effects of edaphic (soil and topography), climatic, and anthropic (cultural practices, ecosystem management, in particular training systems and pruning techniques) factors;

- The production approach in vineyard management, influenced by the incidence of pests and grapevine diseases, water availability, nutrient status, and abiotic stress;
- The natural mutations accumulated in cells over the years through cyclical growth of the plant's permanent structure.

Healthy old vines, and particularly healthy old vineyards, demonstrate the effectiveness of sustainable viticultural practices. They serve as examples of resilience and adaptability to environmental changes and also contribute to the preservation of viticultural landscapes. Given that only a small number of vineyards reach advanced age, studies focusing on the factors that determine longevity and productive potential (yield and quality) are still limited. There is significant room for further research, especially to investigate the elements that promote longevity and a stable relationship between yield and quality.

A precise definition of "Old Vine" and "Old Vineyard" is essential to encourage study, protection, and valorization of these vineyard systems.

- An "Old Vine" is an individual grapevine whose officially documented age is at least thirty-five years. It is the result of a physiological and environmental process that occurred over time, either naturally or intentionally induced (by human factors), allowing the vine to survive in a specific location. In the case of grafted vines, the graft union between scion and rootstock must have remained intact for at least thirty-five years.
- An "Old Vineyard" is a legally delimited, continuous parcel of planted land in which at least 85% of the vines meet the above definition and from which vitivinicultural products are obtained that are eligible to receive legal certification by a competent authority. Its genetic, economic, socio-cultural, and historical characteristics give distinctive features to the grapes and the wines produced.

Through this resolution, the OIV recommends fundamental guidelines for harmonizing evaluation criteria and provides its Member States with a set of recommendations for the analysis and promotion of old vines and vineyards.

4. OIV Definition and Recommendations on the Importance of Mountain and Steep Slope Viticulture for the Vitivinicultural Sector – OIV-VITI 716-2024

Mountain areas and territories characterized by steep slopes are among the most historically and culturally rich agricultural production sites in the world, shaping landscapes that are, in many respects, unique. These vineyards represent a heritage that must be preserved. Mountains are essential sources of water, energy, and biodiversity. However, they suffer from accelerated soil erosion, are prone to landslides, and face rapid loss of habitat and genetic diversity. Studies indicate an increasing impact from the combined effects of climate change and unsustainable intensification of agricultural exploitation. Mountain viticulture plays a crucial role in reducing erosion, landslides, and the downstream effects of flooding. The mountain environment can reduce pathogen pressure on vines while simultaneously enhancing wine quality. These vineyards also represent a significant economic activity in frequently disadvantaged areas.

Mountain and steep slope climates, thanks to better sunlight exposure in spring and autumn due to the orientation of slopes, may be a key factor in achieving full grape ripening in certain high-altitude wine regions. However, this form of viticulture faces two primary threats: cost and climate.

- It has always been more expensive than viticulture in flat areas, and the cost gap has widened with the increasing mechanization of level vineyards.
- In some regions, climate change may turn the once-beneficial climatic conditions of steep slopes into disadvantages. Depending on soil composition and geographic location—particularly in warmer regions—greater solar radiation can pose challenges. Reduced water retention capacity and high evapotranspiration often result in water stress that lowers yields. Erosion and soil loss are intensified by changing rainfall patterns and the increased frequency of extreme weather events. These frequent intense rainfalls can lead to severe erosion and landslides, heightening the risk of both material damage and human loss. South-facing slopes may experience earlier vegetation cycles and are at high risk for damage caused by late frosts.

Although producers generally express positive outlooks and attitudes, consumer awareness of the products and ecosystem services offered by this type of viticulture remains limited.

The OIV has adopted the following definition: "Mountain and steep slope viticulture" refers to vineyard systems planted in mountainous areas, understood as land located at high altitudes, on steep slopes, or in topographically rugged zones, according to scientific criteria proposed by the UNEP-WCMC (UN Environment Programme World Conservation Monitoring Centre) and the identification methodology developed by Eurostat.

The OIV recommends that Member States promote, support, analyze, and study the preservation of this form of viticulture as an important heritage and income source for the wine sector, as well as a provider of ecosystem services to local communities—namely, water conservation, soil preservation, and biodiversity protection.

5. Use of Fumaric Acid for Wine Acidification – OIV-OENO 581B-2024

Available data demonstrate that fumaric acid can be used to correct wine defects and, in particular, to lower its pH, albeit with limitations due to its low solubility in water and, consequently, in polar solutions such as wine. The use of fumaric acid in wine is authorised by several regulatory frameworks, and wines treated with fumaric acid are marketed internationally across multiple countries. Moreover, acidification can contribute to a reduction in the SO_2 content of wines.

Therefore, based on a proposal by Commission II "Oenology", the OIV has decided to add "fumaric acid" (as an additive) to the list of authorised compounds in the "chemical acidification" sheet of the OIV International Code of Oenological Practices. As a result, the classification and regulation are updated to state that the only acids whose use is authorised are: lactic, L(–) or D,L-malic, L(+)-tartaric, fumaric, and citric acids.

6. Treatment with Functionalised Mesoporous Silica (FMS) for Protein Stabilisation of Wines – OIV-OENO 672B-2024

Having assessed its technological properties, Functionalised Mesoporous Silica (FMS) is to be considered a processing aid and has been included in the OIV International Code of Oenological Practices for the selective absorption and removal of unstable proteins present in wine, under the following conditions of use:

- The treatment may be carried out in tank by batch method (static clarification) or through a continuous system by passing the wine over a layer of FMS (percolation). The regeneration of FMS allows for its reuse.

- The dosage, to be determined through preliminary testing, is approximately 10–150 g/hL.
- No preparation phase (e.g., rehydration) is required. In the case of batch treatment, FMS can be added directly to the wine, with homogenisation achieved through pump-over.
- After treatment, the wine must be filtered through a filtration medium with pore diameter not exceeding 0.45 µm.
- The FMS used must comply with the specifications of the OIV International Oenological Codex.

7. Update to the Monograph and Codex on Plant Protein Substances (Removal of Wheat) – OIV-OENO 723-2024

In light of the work carried out by the "Food Safety" Expert Group, and in particular the recommendation concerning the potential allergenic risk posed by wheat proteins used as a fining agent in wine, and considering that alternative plant-based protein substances (derived from peas and potatoes) are available for the same purpose, the OIV has decided to remove "plant protein substances extracted from wheat as a technological processing aid" from its Codex and monographs.

8. Update to the Monographs on Primary and Secondary Products of Non-Saccharomyces Yeasts – OIV-OENO 740-2024

It was decided to amend previous Resolutions with the following new texts: Mannoproteins are extracted from the cell walls of *Saccharomyces* spp. or non-*Saccharomyces* yeasts using physicochemical or enzymatic methods. The proteins in yeast protein extracts originate mainly from the cytoplasm of *Saccharomyces* spp. or non-*Saccharomyces* yeasts. These are produced from biomass of *Saccharomyces* spp. or non-*Saccharomyces* yeasts, inactivated by heat and/or pH variation. They are derived from the biomass of yeasts belonging to the *Saccharomyces* spp. or non-*Saccharomyces* genera. Yeast cell walls are obtained from *Saccharomyces* spp. or non-*Saccharomyces* yeasts.

9. Analytical Parameters Commonly Used for Wines and Sparkling Wines – OIV-OENO 712A-2024

The OIV Assembly, following a proposal by the "Oenology" Commission and the "Methods of Analysis" Subcommission, has decided to replace a section of the *Compendium of International Methods of Analysis of Wines and*

Musts **concerning the rules for applying analytical methods and reporting results.**

For the analytical parameters commonly used for wines and sparkling wines, the applicable rules for the "Methods of Analysis" used in determining these parameters must follow the following order of priority:

- Methods adopted by the OIV and published in the OIV *Compendium of International Methods of Analysis of Wines and Musts*;
- Methods adopted by the International Organization for Standardization (ISO);
- Methods adopted by other standardization bodies.

The analytical parameters commonly used for wines and sparkling wines are essential analytical indicators that allow for a satisfactory verification that the product characteristics comply with the OIV's definitions and oenological practices. These parameters also serve as a basis for commercial transactions. Member States may use other parameters according to their specific needs.

The analytical parameters commonly used for wines and sparkling wines include:

Density at 20 °C (g/cm³)	Alcohol content by volume at 20 °C (% vol)
Sum of glucose and fructose (g/L)	Total sulfur dioxide (mg/L)
Total acidity (mEq/L) or (g tartaric acid/L) or (g sulfuric acid/L)	pH
Volatile acidity (mEq/L) or (g sulfuric acid/L) or (g acetic acid/L)	Sucrose in sparkling and semi-sparkling wines (g/L)
Overpressure of carbon dioxide in sparkling wines (bar)	

10. Determination of Mineral Elements in Grape Juice, Reconstituted Grape Juice, Concentrated Grape Juice, and Grape Nectar – OIV-OENO 662K-2024

For the determination of the content of primary and secondary mineral elements in grape juice, reconstituted grape juice, concentrated grape juice, and grape nectar, it has been approved to add an analytical method using ICP/AES (Inductively Coupled Plasma Atomic Emission Spectrometry).

This determination applies to the following elements:

- **Primary mineral elements**: Potassium, Calcium, Magnesium, and Sodium;
- **Secondary mineral elements**: Iron, Copper, Zinc, Strontium, Aluminum, and Barium.

11. Update to the International Standard for Wine Labelling: Grape Variety Name – OIV-ECO 696-2024

Considering the need to update the requirements for indicating grape variety names on wine labels and to improve the quality of information provided to consumers, it has been decided to amend the International Standard for Wine Labelling by replacing it with the following text:

- "The wine must be made from at least 85% of the named grape variety (excluding any quantity of wine products used for sweetening)." The previous version stated "75%".
- "Where the names of two or more grape varieties or their synonyms are indicated, the product in question must have been obtained from at least 85% of those varieties (excluding any quantity of wine products used for sweetening)." The previous version stated: "the wine must have been entirely obtained from those varieties."
- Wine grape varieties must be indicated on the label in descending order according to the percentage used and must appear in characters of the same size. No grape variety may be mentioned on the label if it was used in a lower proportion than another variety that is not mentioned.

12. Update to the OIV International Standard for Wine Labelling – Electronic Label, Nutritional Declaration, and Ingredient Indication – OIV-ECO 676-2024

Considering consumers' interest in information regarding the composition and nutritional content of wines, the need to harmonize communication rules in order to facilitate international trade, and technological advances concerning how product information is conveyed to consumers, the decision has been made to amend the "General Provisions" of the OIV International Standard for Wine Labelling by adding four new definitions:

- **"Labelling"**: any written, printed, or graphic element appearing on the label, accompanying the wine also in electronic form, or displayed near the product, including promotional content.
- **"Electronic label"**: label (or some of its elements) provided in electronic form.
- **"Ingredient"**: any substance, including food additives, used in the preparation of wine and present in the final product even in a modified form. Processing aids described in the OIV International Code of Oenological Practices and any residual traces thereof are not considered ingredients.
- **"Nutritional declaration"**: a standardised indication or list of the nutrients contained in a food product.

In OIV Member States where allowed, both mandatory and optional information may be provided via an electronic label. In such cases, the physical label must display a clear and direct link specifying which information is provided electronically.

Mandatory and optional information displayed on the electronic label must not be shown alongside any commercial or promotional content. The collection or tracking of any personal/user data is not permitted, unless otherwise specified by applicable national legislation. The direct link to the electronic label on the physical label should be clearly identified using non-textual methods such as pictograms or symbols that are easily visible and readily understandable by consumers.

With this provision, the OIV aligns itself with European regulations, while leaving other Member States the option to restrict the nutritional declaration displayed on the label to the energy value only.

13. Revised OIV Regulation on International Competitions for Wines and Wine-Based Spirits - OIV-OENO 671C-2024

For international competitions, and considering the decision to remove the bronze medal from the award system—as it is deemed less representative than the silver and gold medals—it has been decided to eliminate the awarding of bronze medals from OIV-endorsed competitions.

From now on, medals will be awarded to products achieving at least the following scores (on a 100-point scale):

- **Grand Gold Medal** – minimum of 93 points (previously 92 points)
- **Gold Medal** – minimum of 89 points (previously 85 points)
- **Silver Medal** – minimum of 85 points (previously 82 points)

The **bronze medal**, previously awarded to products scoring at least 80 points in competitions, has been discontinued.

14. Repeal of Obsolete, Outdated and Redundant OIV Resolutions – OIV-ECO 726-2024

Between 1928 and 2023, the OIV adopted a total of 1,432 resolutions. Among these, some have become obsolete, outdated, or redundant and are no longer applicable. It has therefore been decided to repeal 184 resolutions, listed in an annex (not reproduced here), with the aim of improving the coherence of the body of resolutions and facilitating their implementation by the Member States.

The Disputes Regarding Agricultural Lease Contracts in the Italian System of Authorisations for Viticulture Plantations

Fracesco Tedioli
* Agricultural Law Expert Attorney, independent arbitrator and Adjunct Professor of Commercial law at the University of Mantova (Italy).

Summary: 1. Regulation (EU) No. 1308/2013: From the Rights System to Authorisations - 2. European Regulations on Authorisations Following Regulation (EU) No. 2117/2021- 3. The Role of the Regions in the Administration of Authorisations for New Plantations and Replanting – 4. Modification of the Expiration of an Authorisation and Sanctions for Non-use - 5. Issuance of Authorisations for Replanting Following Uprooting - 6. Uprooting Policies and the Current Debate – 7. Modification of the Location of the Area for Which the Authorisation is Granted - 7.1 Intra-company Replanting - 7.2 Inter-company Replanting - 8. Modification of the Reference Region - 9. Fake leases: a significant challenge within the context of authorisation systems. A Contentious Issue - 9.1 Practical Issues and Disputes Related to Sham Leases - 10. Conclusions: The Need for a Balanced Approach

1. Regulation (EU) No. 1308/2013: From the Rights System to Authorisations

The introduction of Regulation (EU) No. 1308/2013[10] marked a significant shift in the system for managing vineyard surfaces. Previously, planting rights[11] could be transferred without the sale of the land on which they were exercised[12]. However, with the advent of this regulation, a new mechanism based on non-transferable administrative authorisations came into effect. These authorisations

10 See Regulation (EU) No. 1308/2013 of the European Parliament and of the Council of 17 December 2013 establishing a common organization of the markets in agricultural products and repealing Council Regulations (EEC) No. 922/72, (EEC) No. 234/79, (EC) No. 1037/2001, and (EC) No. 1234/2007.

11 Also identified in legal doctrine as "production rights"; in France ("*droit à produire*" and "*droit de produire*"). See also Rook Basile, *Introduzione al diritto agrario*, Milan, 1985, p. 86, who defines such rights as "*measures of production*"

12 The legislation stipulated that, by 31 December 2015 (the deadline was subsequently extended to 2025), producers could convert their existing planting rights into authorisations through a market-based transaction, thus avoiding the loss of an intangible asset that is essential for the exercise of agricultural activity.

are subject to a pre-established expiration date and, unlike planting rights, cannot be transferred without the sale of the land in question.

Before the regulation came into force, planting and replanting rights constituted a mechanism through which producers could transfer their rights to third parties[13]. However, this system was susceptible to speculative practices, exemplified by the phenomenon of sham leases, which enabled producers to circumvent the prohibition on the transfer of rights for consideration.

The changes introduced by EU legislation have resulted in the implementation of a more public-centric regulatory framework, centred on authorisations granted by Member States. This has ensured more direct control over vineyard surfaces and prevented speculation in the transfer of rights. The regulatory framework[14] is based on a system that sets production limits and establishes rules for planting new vineyards or uprooting old ones, followed by the replanting of new vines. The objective is to ensure orderly vineyard growth that can respond to the anticipated increase in global market demand[15].

As of 1 January 2016, the legislation pertaining to planting and replanting rights was revoked, along with the associated regulatory framework governing their recognition and transfer[16]. In lieu of the aforementioned provisions, a system was introduced based on the issuance of authorisations by member states or regions[17]. The legislation distinguishes between new vineyard plantings (Articles 63-65 of Regulation No. 1308/2013) and replanting following

13 The legislation stipulated that, by 31 December 2015 (the deadline was subsequently extended to 2025), producers could convert their existing planting rights into authorisations through a market-based transaction, thus avoiding the loss of an intangible asset that is essential for the exercise of agricultural activity.

14 The regulatory framework derived from European legislation regarding planting authorisations in the wine sector is constituted by a variety of sources. In addition to Regulation No. 1308/2013 (Arts. 61 et seq.), the regulatory framework also encompasses delegated and implementing acts, as well as several domestic provisions, including the Unified Wine Law, particularly with regard to sanctions. Furthermore, secondary legislation and various technical provisions contained in ministerial or AGEA circulars relating to the operational procedures for the issuance of authorisations constitute an integral part of the regulatory framework. For further details on the implementation in Italy, please refer to Sequino, Bonifazi, and Apollonio, *La nuova normativa vitivinicola. Tracciabilità, semplificazione, autocontrollo dopo il Testo unico del vino*, Milan, 2019, pp. 113 et seq.

15 On this matter, see Caviglia, *Manuale di diritto vitivinicolo*, Rome, 2017, pp. 121 et seq.

16 Art. 61 of Regulation (EU) No. 1308/2013.

17 The aim of EU legislation is to increase the competitiveness of wine in the global market by allowing the establishment of new plantings, while preventing an excessively rapid increase in vineyard plantings in response to rising demand, which could result in oversupply with social and environmental repercussions in specific wine-growing areas. On this point, see Lucifero, *Il sistema di autorizzazioni per gli impianti viticoli: il regime vigente e la riforma dell'Ocm post 2020*, in *Riv. dir. agr.*, 2020, p. 262.

uprooting or anticipated uprooting (Article 66). In the case of the latter, an authorisation must be issued by the relevant Member State upon the request of the interested producer, free of charge (Article 62).

The granting of authorisations[18] is permitted for the establishment of new vineyard areas or for replanting, with a maximum limit of 1% of the total national vineyard surface[19]. This figure is subject to annual revision based on market conditions. Periodic reviews of this figure are conducted, with the possibility of further extensions or modifications depending on market conditions[20].

Furthermore, the system of authorisations is augmented by the Commission Delegated Regulation (EU) No. 273/2018 and the Implementing Regulation (EU) No. 274/2018.

2. European Regulations on Authorisations Following Regulation (EU) No. 2117/2021

As previously stated, Regulation (EU) No. 2117/2021[21], which updates the 2013 Regulation, introduces significant alterations to the Authorisation management system in accordance with the objectives of the 2023-2027 Common Agricultural Policy (CAP)[22]. Notwithstanding certain variations and additions, the regulatory model has remained largely unchanged and has even been extended in temporal application.

The recently implemented authorisation system, which provides authorisations free of charge to producers and has a three-year validity period if unused, has been designed with the objective of mitigating market turbulence caused by the

18 The issuing of planting and replanting authorisations, within the framework of administrative measures, permits the exercise of a specific activity by the entrepreneur on the basis of a discretionary, rather than technical, assessment by the Public Administration.

19 The aforementioned reference pertains to the vineyard area that existed in the previous year.

20 The principal objective is to avert an excess supply that could imperil the economic stability of the sector.

21 The Regulation of the European Parliament and of the Council of 2 December 2021, No. 2117/2021, published in the Official Journal of the European Union on 6 December 2021, No. L 435/262, amends Regulation (EU) No. 1308/2013, which establishes a common organisation of the markets in agricultural products. The following Regulations are also relevant: EU No. 1151/2012 on quality schemes for agricultural products and foodstuffs, Regulation (EU) No. 251/2014 concerning the definition, designation, presentation, labelling, and protection of geographical indications of aromatised wine products, and Regulation (EU) No. 228/2013 laying down specific measures for agriculture in the outermost regions of the Union.

22 The period between 2023 and 2027 will see the implementation of a series of measures designed to promote environmentally friendly viticulture practices. These measures will provide incentives for producers who adopt sustainable practices.

pandemic and other global economic factors. Furthermore, the legislation stipulates that producers who fail to plant within the specified period are subject to sanctions established by European[23] and national regulations[24].

It is important to note, however, that authorisations expiring in 2024 and 2025 can be extended on a regional basis to avoid the forced uprooting of crops in cases of economic hardship for producers. Additionally, the validity of authorisations has been extended to six years in cases of replanting on the same plot or on equivalent plots to those from which uprooting took place.

Article 63 establishes a safeguard mechanism, whereby Member States may issue new authorisations on an annual basis, up to a maximum of 1% of the total vineyard surface within their respective territories, as calculated on 31 July of the preceding year[25]. It should be noted that vineyard areas intended for wine grape production and those that cannot be converted into vineyards under applicable national regulations are excluded from the eligibility assessment.

Furthermore, Regulation (EU) No. 2117/2021 requires that Member States, using the vineyard register[26], submit an updated inventory of their productive potential to the European Commission by 1 March of each year if their national plans include measures for restructuring and converting vineyards[27].

Additionally, producers who commit to uprooting an equivalent surface by the conclusion of the fourth year may be granted automatic authorisation.

With regard to replanting, Article 66 of the Single CMO Regulation stipulates that an authorisation shall be issued automatically upon request for an area equivalent to that previously uprooted. The authorisation must be used on the same farm where the uprooting occurred. Authorisation may also be granted automatically to producers who commit to uprooting an equivalent surface by the end of the fourth year from the date of planting the new vines[28].

23 Art. 89 (4), EU Reg. No 1306/2013.

24 Art. 69 (3) Italian Law No. 238/2016.

25 As previously stated, the area under vines that are currently not eligible for conversion can be included in the aforementioned land.

26 In particular, each vineyard unit deemed suitable for the cultivation of wine grapes is entered into the register, as are the suitability of vineyards for the production of grapes suitable for DOCG, DOC and IG wines. The register is managed by the regions electronically, through the Sian (National Agricultural Information System) service, on the basis of data contained in the company dossier, which must also be prepared electronically by each company in the sector.

27 For further details, please refer to Article 145(3) of EU Regulation No. 1308/2013, as amended by Article 6(1) of EU Regulation No. 2117/2021.

28 The objective of this initiative is to provide assistance to winegrowers who are seeking to renew their plantings.

3. The Role of the Regions in the Administration of Authorisations for New Plantations and Replanting

The regions also play a pivotal role in determining the available areas for new plantations and in communicating this information to the European Commission. In Italy, the responsibility for the management of authorisations is devolved to the Regions. These bodies receive and evaluate applications for new plantations and replanting[29]. On an annual basis, producers who wish to plant new vineyards are required to submit a request to the relevant regional authorities. These authorities oversee the process in accordance with national and European directives. Additionally, the Regions are tasked with determining the available surfaces for new plantations, which they must subsequently communicate to the European Commission.

In particular, the "Unified Text on Wine"[30] establishes that authorisations may be sought for both new plantations[31] and replanting[32], and it also prescribes the mandatory registration of vineyards in the vineyard register. Applications for new plantation authorisations are deemed admissible if the applicant's updated and validated farm file demonstrates that the applicant's agricultural area under management (exclusive of areas subject to restrictions) is equal to or greater than the area for which authorisation is sought[33].

The process is divided into two distinct phases: the regional phase and the national phase. Subsequent to their electronic submission to the relevant regional authority, applications are subject to a discretionary assessment by the

29 In accordance with Article Article 62(4) of EU Regulation No. 1308/2013 states that the authorisation system does not apply to the planting or replanting of areas intended for experimental purposes or for the purpose of establishing a collection of vine varieties for the preservation of genetic resources. Genetic resources or for the cultivation of graft nurseries, areas the wine or vine products of which are intended solely for the consumption of the wine-grower's family, or areas to be used for new planting as a result of expropriation measures in the public interest under national law.

30The legislative instrument in question is Law No. 238 of 12 December 2016, entitled 'Organic regulation of vine cultivation and wine production and trade'. It was published in the Official Gazette No. 302 of 28 December 2016.

31 In the case of new plants, the authorisation process is based on a predetermined ceiling, which is calculated according to the available surfaces. This ceiling is determined by nationally defined priority and threshold criteria that regulate the allocation of new surfaces.

32 In the case of replanting authorisations, which do not result in the recognition of a new vineyard area, but correspond to an area equivalent to that of the previously grubbed-up area within the holding, the individual regions automatically recognise the relevant changes.

33 Areas on which there are constraints (environmental, archaeological, landscape, historical, etc.) that are not evident from the farm file and that would prevent their conversion into vineyards are excluded. In the case of applications in more than one region, this eligibility criterion must be verified in each of these regions, i.e. the holding must have an agricultural area in each region equal to or greater than that for which it is applying in the same region. .

Ministry of Agriculture (Masaf) in regard to the allocation of authorisations and the potential application of priority criteria in instances where the volume of requests exceeds the available annual surface area. Subsequently, the issuing of the authorisation is conducted by the relevant regional authorities[34].

Furthermore, in order to guarantee the quality of the product, the regions may, at the recommendation of the protection consortia and following consultation with the most representative professional and trade organisations, regulate the registration of vineyards in the vineyard register for the purpose of claiming the related Denominations of Origin (DO) or Geographical Indications (GI). This is done with the aim of ensuring market balance[35]. Consequently, the regions are empowered to regulate vineyard registration in the aforementioned register, with the objective of promoting grape varieties that are destined for the production of DOP or IGP wines, as well as those that fall within the Italian DOCG, DOC, or IGT categories.

The granting of authorisations is free of charge and non-transferable between producers, irrespective of whether they possess the land in question. Nevertheless, there are exceptions to this rule, including cases of inheritance and early succession, company mergers or divisions, marriage or civil union, divorce, or the dissolution of civil unions. In such instances, the Ministry will evaluate each case individually[36].

In particular, in the event of the transfer of authorisation as a consequence of the death of the original recipient, the heir may utilise it for the remainder of its validity period[37].

This exception does not apply in cases of long-term professional incapacity, given that the authorisation does not necessitate the planting to be carried out by the producer in person.

---

34 The Ministry is required to communicate the availability of new planting authorisations in the electronic system within SIAN to the relevant Regions/PP.AA. by 10 July of each year. The list of companies to which these authorisations are to be issued must also be made available. The central system automatically generates the authorisations in the Register, one for each region indicated in the application, by setting the 'reference region'. The regions will issue the authorisations by 1 August using special functions available on the applications, and the authorisations will be made visible to the producer in the dedicated area of their own company file on the SIAN portal.

35 Art. 39, l. n. 238/2016.

36 The cited exceptions are elucidated in the provisions of Ministerial Circular No. 5852 of 25 October 2016.

37 The same principle applies in cases of 'anticipated testamentary succession'. In such instances, the heir is bound by the same criteria that determined the granting of the authorisation.

A further case concerns mergers or divisions, whereby the company in possession of the requisite authorisation is no longer able to maintain its legal personality. The newly constituted entity or the companies resulting from the division shall assume all rights and obligations, including those previously granted authorisations.

The transfer of authorisation is contingent upon the sale of the business, which should be accompanied by the transfer of the authorisation to the purchaser. However, this limitation on the circulation of authorisation can be overcome in the case of an agricultural company, whereby the company shares may be transferred to another party after obtaining the authorisation, thereby transferring the entire business structure, including the authorisation.

4. Modification of the Expiration of an Authorisation and Sanctions for Non-use

It is incumbent upon the vineyard producer to notify the relevant regional authority of the total or partial use of the authorisation within 60 days of planting, irrespective of the type of authorisation in question.

It is noteworthy that the Supreme Court has recently ruled that failure to notify the regional authority of the use of the authorisation for a new planting constitutes a serious violation, rather than merely an administrative irregularity. Such an omission renders the acquisition of the requisite rights to plant the vineyard unlawful[38].

It is a requirement that authorisations are used within the period of validity, otherwise administrative sanctions will be applied in accordance with. Article 69 of the Unified Wine Law.

It is not permitted to modify the duration of authorisations in the event of force majeure, except in the case of replanting on the same uprooted areas[39].

A producer who fails to utilise an authorisation for new plantings within the specified validity period is liable to face the following administrative sanctions[40]:

1. In the event of non-compliance, the producer shall be excluded from the support measures provided by the Common Organization of the Wine Market (OCM) for a period of three years, in addition to being subject to a

38 Court of Cassation, Civil Division II, Order of 15 February 2024, No. 4188.

39 See Article 62, paragraph 2 of Regulation (EU) No. 1308/2013 as amended by Article 1, paragraph 10, letter (a) of Regulation (EU) 2021/2117.

40In compliance with Article 69 (violations related to wine-growing potential) of the Consolidated Wine Law under Law No. 238 of 12 December 2016, and specifically pursuant to paragraph 3.

fine of 1,500 euros per hectare, if the planted area is less than or equal to 20% of the total area granted with the aforementioned authorisation.

2. In the event that the planted area exceeds 20% but does not exceed 60% of the total area granted with the authorisation, the producer shall be excluded from the support measures provided by the OCM for a period of two years, and shall also be subject to a fine of 1,000 euros per hectare.

3. Furthermore, exclusion from the support measures provided by the OCM and a fine of 500 euros per hectare will be imposed if the planted area is greater than 60% but less than the total area granted with the aforementioned authorisation.

In the event of failure to utilise the authorisation for an area of less than one hectare, no proportional reduction of the applicable sanction is foreseen. Nevertheless, in the event that the unplanted area is less than 5% of the total area granted with the aforementioned authorisation, and in any case does not exceed 0.5 hectares, no sanction shall be applied[41]. In the case of authorised areas of less than 0.3 hectares, the aforementioned percentage is increased to 10%.

In the event of a producer relinquishing a granted authorisation subsequent to receiving an area that is less than 100% but greater than 50% of the initially requested area, in accordance with the stipulations set forth in Commission Implementing Regulation (EU) 2018/274 of 11 December 2017, an administrative fine of 500 euros per hectare or fraction thereof of the authorised area will be imposed, in addition to exclusion from the OCM support measures for a period of two years[42].

The authority to impose sanctions is vested in the regions. The recognition of force majeure or exceptional circumstances, as provided by the current EU and national regulations, entails exemption from the application of sanctions. Furthermore, no sanctions will be applied in instances where errors in the completion of the authorisation request are the result of factors beyond the control of the applicant, such as system errors or errors on the part of the processing authority.

5. Issuance of Authorisations for Replanting Following Uprooting

A replanting permit may be granted by the relevant region to a vineyard operator who has removed a portion of their vineyard and submitted a formal request for such authorisation. The aforementioned authorisations are valid for a period of three years from the date of issuance.

41 Refer to paragraph 4 of the above-cited legislation.

42 See paragraph 5 of the aforementioned legislation.

The replanting authorisation request must be submitted by the end of the second growing season following the uprooting; otherwise, the authorisation will not be issued. In the event that replanting is to occur on the same area where the uprooting took place, the producer may avail themselves of a simplified procedure, provided that replanting occurs within 3 years of the uprooting.
Nevertheless, should the producer elect to replant on a different area or within the three-year period subsequent to the issuance of the authorisation, the standard procedure must be adhered to. In such instances, the producer is obliged to submit a notice of completed uprooting no later than the conclusion of the growing season in which the uprooting occurred[43]. This notice will be recorded in the Uprooted Areas Registry for regions operating through the National Agricultural Information System (SIAN), or in the respective information system of other regions, and will serve as a prerequisite for the replanting authorisation request.
The replanting authorisation request must be submitted by the end of the second growing season following the uprooting; otherwise, the authorisation will not be granted.
Following the issuance of replanting authorisations subsequent to uprooting, those granted in accordance with the provisions of EU Regulation 2021/2117 may be utilised for a period of up to six years from the date of issuance, provided that the replanting is conducted on the same vineyard area where the uprooting was carried out. In the event that the replanting is undertaken on a different area, the aforementioned authorisation must be utilised within three years from the date of issuance.
The additional clarification provided by case law is that vineyard replanting, which is defined as an agricultural land movement, does not require the acquisition of building or landscape permits. This ruling[44] has reduced the bureaucratic burdens faced by producers, facilitating the replanting process without the need for additional permits.

6. Uprooting Policies and the Current Debate

One of the most significant challenges currently facing the wine industry is the issue of vineyard uprooting policies. These policies are often regarded as an effective measure to address the problem of overproduction. However, these agronomic practices are the subject of criticism from numerous producers' associations, which express concerns about the potential negative effects on biodiversity and territorial identity.

43 In the absence of specific regional provisions, the aforementioned provisions shall prevail.
44 See. T.A.R. Toscana, Florence, Sec. III, 8 May 2019, no. 684.

Although uprooting is presented as a solution to limit excess production, it risks not only compromising product quality and the economic sustainability of wine businesses but also significantly altering the wine landscape. The reduction in crop diversity could, in fact, impoverish the biological and cultural diversity that characterises many Italian wine-growing areas, with potential repercussions on wine tourism and the overall image of the sector on a global scale.

7. Modification of the Location of the Area for Which the Authorisation is Granted

The high number of applications submitted annually by producers has progressively reduced the available areas for the establishment of new vineyards, thereby highlighting critical issues within the authorisation circulation system. This phenomenon has given rise to concerns related to the limitation of vineyard areas and the management of authorisations[45].

7.1 Intra-company Replanting

In order to expand the cultivated area of a vineyard, intra-company replanting authorisations have frequently been employed.

In the event that a planting authorisation is granted for the same area that has been uprooted, the modification of the area is not permitted from the third year onwards, given that the authorisation has a duration of six years.

In the event that the business is also conducted on land leased from others under a rental agreement, the transfer of the replanting authorisation may extend to these additional lands, even if they are different from the uprooted areas, on the grounds that they form part of the same agricultural business. Nevertheless, it is essential that the rental agreement be drawn up in accordance with Article 45 of Law No. 203 of 1982 provides for the return of leased land without the vineyard, thus allowing for a change in the designated use of the plots that were uprooted.

Moreover, the vineyard planted subsequent to the issuance of the authorisation must be maintained for a minimum of five years, except in cases of force majeure or phytosanitary reasons. Consequently, the uprooting of vineyards planted with new planting authorisations prior to the expiration of five years from the planting date does not result in the issuance of replanting authorisations[46].

45 This phenomenon is particularly pronounced in regions that are especially conducive to wine production.

46 See. Agea, '*Criteri di ammissibilità*', p. 16, National Implementing Provisions DM 649010 of 19 December 2022 on the authorisation system for vine planting referred to in Regulation (EU) No 1308/2013 of the European Parliament and of the Council.

Furthermore, case law has elucidated that the sole prerequisite for the issuance of a vineyard replanting authorization is that the land in question remains accessible to the applicant subsequent to the authorized uprooting. Additional business justifications cannot be invoked to justify the denial of the authorization. This reaffirms the significance of a transparent and impartial application of the regulations, thereby limiting the discretionary powers of the competent authorities[47].

7.2 Inter-company Replanting

A distinct scenario arises when, at the applicant's request, a vineyard is planted in an area distinct from the one for which the authorisation was initially granted. This practice is permitted only if the new area meets the same conditions for which the authorisation was originally issued, including any priority criteria[48].

8. Modification of the Reference Region

In the event that a change to the reference region is required for authorisations related to uprooting, the relevant request must be submitted to the region where the new planting is to take place. In order to proceed with this request, it is necessary to obtain the consent of both the region where the planting is intended and the region from which the authorisation originates.

In the event that the region where the planting is intended raises no objections, the aforementioned region must contact the administration that granted the aforementioned authorisation. This administration must then verify whether the aforementioned authorisation is still valid and whether it was granted based on territorial eligibility criteria or other restrictions that would prevent a change of reference region.

Nevertheless, the reference region may not be altered for authorisations pertaining to early replanting. Furthermore, the uprooting of vineyards conducted prior to the expiration of six years from the date of registration of the temporary management transfer does not result in the issuance of new replanting authorisations in a region other than the one where the uprooting took place

This provision also applies in instances where requests are made to transfer a replanting authorisation for leased land in a region different from the one of origin, where the lease has been in effect for a period of less than six years[49].

---

47 T.A.R. Sicilia, Palermo, Sec. II, 17 March 2020, no. 635.

48 See Agea, cited in article 4.

49 It should be noted that this provision does not apply to temporary transfer deeds that were registered prior to 21 March 2018. This date marks the entry into force of Ministerial Decree No. 935 of 13 February 2018.

9. Fake leases: a significant challenge within the context of authorisation systems. A Contentious Issue

One of the most significant challenges that has arisen within the authorisation system is the phenomenon of fake leases[50]. This practice has, in fact, resulted in a distortion of the original purpose of replanting authorisations, which are not intended to increase vineyard areas but to renew them.

Fake leases are agreements whereby authorisations are transferred from one region to another, frequently a considerable distance away, with the sole intention of exploiting vineyard areas for replanting in a different location.

In response to this growing phenomenon, the European Commission has clarified that leasing of vineyard areas with the exclusive intent to immediately uproot and replant elsewhere, based on short-term contracts, cannot be considered a legitimate agricultural activity. In particular, if the area in question has not been managed by the lessee for an appropriate period, it is evident that the intention is to circumvent the principles of non-transferability and free-of-charge authorisations. Such actions erode the integrity of the authorisation system, which was devised to guarantee transparency and the proper administration of vineyard areas[51].

Notwithstanding the formal prohibition of such practices, fake leases have continued to proliferate due to a lack of effective oversight, resulting in distortions and abuses within the system. In accordance with Regulation (EU) No. 1308/2013, the transfer of authorisations is subject to strict limitations, with the stipulation that planting rights cannot be transferred without meeting specific requirements.

In consequence of this intervention, the legislature was obliged to amend the pertinent regulations, thereby requiring that vineyards planted under authorisation must be maintained for a minimum period of five years. Consequently, the uprooting of vineyards prior to the expiration of six years from the date of registration of the lease contract does not entitle the lessee to a new replanting authorisation in a region different from that in which the uprooting occurred[52].

---

50 Prior to the implementation of the revised regulations, these contractual instruments were utilized by producers as a conduit for surreptitious transfer of replanting rights, effectively circumventing the stipulations pertaining to the onerous transfer of rights. This strategy enabled the lessee to reap the benefits of the rights without being subjected to the penalties prescribed by the now-repealed legislation.

51 See European Commission Opinion Ares (2017) 5680223 of 21 November 2017.

52 MiPaaF Ministerial Decree, 13 February 2018, n 935 amending MiPaaF Ministerial Decree, 15 December 2015, n 12272.

9.1 Practical Issues and Disputes Related to Fake Leases

The existence of fake leases in the wine sector gives rise to a number of legal issues that may emerge during the course of the lease agreement or at its conclusion. The following section enumerates some of the most common issues.

1. **Landlord's refusal to sign consent for uprooting**

   In the event that, subsequent to the signing of the lease agreement, the landlord declines to sign the consent for uprooting, which is a prerequisite for the transfer of replanting rights from one plot to another, this constitutes a breach of contract. In such cases, the lessee may pursue the forced performance of the contract or, alternatively, terminate the contract and seek damages. If the contract specifically provides for uprooting and the transfer of rights, the landlord's refusal could be considered a serious breach, justifying a claim for damages.

2. **Compensation for expenses incurred by the lessee**

   In the event that the lessee has planted new vineyards or renovated existing ones during the term of the lease, the question of compensation may arise at the conclusion of the lease. The Unified Law on Agricultural Leases (Law No. 203/1982) stipulates that the lessee is entitled to compensation for improvements made, as set forth in Article 17. In the event that such improvements have increased the value of the land.

3. **Non-renewal of the lease or failure to sell the land**

   In the event that the landlord does not intend to renew the lease with the lessee who has planted new vineyards, or does not intend to sell the land to the lessee, the situation becomes more complex, particularly in regard to the lessee's investment. In such cases, it is of the utmost importance that the contract contains a clause that stipulates the fate of the improvements made to the land at the conclusion of the lease. In the absence of such a stipulation, the lessee may be liable to forfeit the investment made.

4. **Fake leases and excessive rent**

   Another common issue with fake lease agreements is the imposition of an excessively high rent in comparison to similar leases. In instances where leases are drawn up with the intention of circumventing regulations that prohibit the charging of fees for the transfer of replanting rights, the contract term is frequently limited to a period of three years, and the rent is set at an excessive rate. In such cases, the contract may be deemed null or voidable due to an illegal cause, as it violates current regulations. Furthermore, the courts may interpret the disproportionate rent as evidence of a sham transaction, potentially declaring the contract null and restoring the original situation.

10. Conclusions: The Need for a Balanced Approach

The authorisation system for vineyard plantings represents a pivotal instrument for the governance and oversight of the wine sector in Italy and the European Union. Nevertheless, considerable challenges remain, particularly with regard to the issue of fictitious leases and uprooting policies. These require ongoing regulatory updates and careful oversight.

The role of jurisprudence in clarifying various aspects of this system has been pivotal. In the future, it will be crucial to maintain a balance between the necessity to regulate the market and the importance of protecting producers' rights. This will ensure that uprooting policies or evasive practices, such as fake leases, do not undermine the credibility and sustainability of the wine sector.

The CAP 2023-2027 offers significant opportunities for the promotion of sustainable and high-quality wine production. Nevertheless, it is of the utmost importance that national and regional authorities rigorously enforce the new regulations, while ensuring that producers receive the necessary support to adapt to changes. It is only through a balanced approach, combining regulation and flexibility, that the long-term success and sustainable growth of the wine sector can be ensured.

Agricultural Contracts, Production Costs, and Unfair Trading Practices: The Sale of Grapes Between Regulation and Critical Issues

Fracesco Tedioli
* Agricultural Law Expert Attorney, independent arbitrator and Adjunct Professor of Commercial law at the University of Mantova (Italy).

Summary:1) Regulatory Developments in the Sale of Agricultural and Food Products: From Decree-Law No. 1/2012 to Legislative Decree No. 198/2021; 2) Material and Personal Scope of the Current Legal Framework; 3)The Requirement of Written Form and the Essential Content of Supply Contracts;4) The Sale of Grapes and Must: General Rules and Sector-Specific Provisions; 5) The Amendments Introduced by Decree-Law No. 63/2024 on Unfair Trading Practices; 6) The Critical Tension Between Contractual Freedom and Regulatory Constraints in Price Determination; 7) Sanctions, Remedial Mechanisms, and the Impact on Supply Chain Organisation; 8) Critical Reflections and Systemic Perspectives.

1. Regulatory Developments Concerning the Sale of Agricultural and Food Products: From Decree-Law No. 1/2012 to Legislative Decree No. 198/2021

The regulatory framework governing commercial practices in transactions involving agricultural and food products has undergone a significant evolution, culminating in the adoption of **Legislative Decree No. 198 of 8 November 2021**[53].

This legislative measure was enacted in implementation of **Directive (EU) 2019/633** on unfair trading practices in business-to-business relationships in the agricultural and food supply chain. The decree aims to introduce more effective regulatory tools that are better aligned with the operational realities of Italian agricultural enterprises, thereby ensuring stronger protection for the weaker contractual party, in accordance with the principles underpinning the EU legal order.

53**Legislative Decree No. 198 of 8 November 2021**, which officially entered into force on **15 December 2021**, repealed the previous regulatory framework set out in **Article 62 of Decree-Law No. 1 of 24 January 2012**, converted, with amendments, by **Law No. 27 of 24 March 2012**.

Within this framework, the Italian legislature pursued a dual objective: on the one hand, to **strengthen contractual balance** within agro-food supply relationships, and on the other, to **simplify and rationalise** the applicable legal framework, making it clearer, more systematic, and consistent with the principles of **market transparency and fair competition**.

2. Material and Personal Scope of Application of the Current Regulatory Framework

Legislative Decree No. 198 of 8 November 2021, entitled *"Provisions on Unfair Trading Practices in Business Relationships within the Agricultural and Food Supply Chain"*, significantly broadened both the **personal and material scope** of the discipline, compared to the previous regulatory framework established by Article 62 of Decree-Law No. 1/2012. This expansion is particularly significant in that it directly affects the **classification of contractual relationships** within the supply chain, involving categories of agricultural and agri-industrial operators that were previously excluded from the specific regulation of unfair practices.

From a **personal standpoint**, the new legal regime applies not only to relationships between agricultural undertakings and commercial or industrial enterprises, but also to **transactions between farmers**, thereby overcoming the earlier model that restricted the scope to vertical relationships between agricultural suppliers and industrial or retail buyers. As a consequence, even a farmer acting as a purchaser—regardless of their position within the value chain—is now required to comply with the provisions of Legislative Decree No. 198/2021. This has important **practical and systemic implications** in terms of contractual compliance and legal responsibility.

From a **material standpoint**, the decree covers all sales of agricultural and food products **made by operators established in Italy**, regardless of the location of the buyer. This legislative choice **breaks with the previous principle of territoriality**, under which national rules applied only to transactions physically carried out within Italian territory. Under the new framework, **the fact that the seller is established in Italy** is sufficient to trigger the applicability of the decree, even if the buyer is located in another EU Member State or in a third country.

This expansion entails not merely a **quantitative increase**, but a **qualitative transformation** of the regulatory perimeter, clearly reflecting the need to **harmonise protection standards at the European level**, while allowing

Member States to define additional unfair practices beyond those minimally harmonised by **Directive (EU) 2019/633**.

However, as clarified in **Article 1(2)** of the Decree, certain types of transactions are **expressly excluded** from the scope of application. These include:

30. instant sales in which payment is made simultaneously with delivery;
31. sales to final consumers, provided the buyer is not an operator active in the agri-food supply chain; and
32. deliveries by agricultural or fisheries producers to cooperatives or producer organisations **of which they are members**.

This last exclusion deserves closer scrutiny. In the case of **mutualistic contributions** (*conferimenti*), the rationale for the exemption lies in the presumed **contractual symmetry between the member and the cooperative**, grounded in the associative bond and the member's participation in the governance of the collective entity. Nonetheless, case law and part of the legal scholarship have raised doubts about the **actual parity of bargaining power**, especially in the context of large cooperatives with complex organisational structures and concentrated decision-making authority.

It should also be noted that the scope of the decree extends to **atypical contractual arrangements**, such as framework agreements, letters of intent, or ongoing commercial relations not formalised in writing, **provided that the facts indicate the existence of a genuine supply relationship** in the agricultural or food sector. This functional interpretation is consistent with the legislator's intention to **prevent abusive practices** even in flexible contractual settings, without being constrained by classical contractual typologies.

3. The Requirement of Written Form and the Essential Content of Agricultural Product Supply Contracts

One of the key features of **Legislative Decree No. 198/2021** is the imposition of a **written form requirement** for contracts governing the sale of agricultural and food products. This requirement, whose breach results in relative nullity (which may only be asserted by the supplier), reflects the legislator's intent to ensure **transparency, traceability, and legal certainty** within contractual relationships throughout the agri-food supply chain. The regulation is clearly designed to protect the seller, who is structurally deemed to be the weaker party in such transactions, by mandating a formalised agreement that guarantees clarity and verifiability of contractual terms.

The written form may take the shape of an **individual contract**, a **framework agreement** in the case of ongoing or recurring commercial relations, or a **standard-form contract** negotiated with the assistance of the most representative professional organisations at the national level. In any case, the agreement must be **concluded prior to the delivery of goods**, in line with the principle of anteriority, which aims to safeguard the integrity and mutuality of the contracting parties' declarations of intent.

Regardless of the contractual form adopted, the contract must include a **set of essential elements** specified by the decree. First and foremost, the parties must clearly identify the **organoleptic characteristics** of the goods being sold, including whether or not the product is perishable. These characteristics may be directly included in the body of the contract or set out in an annex that forms an integral part of the agreement. The **quantity of the goods** must also be specified, either precisely or in approximate terms, provided that the final quantity is later ascertainable through supplementary documentation such as purchase orders, delivery notes, or invoices.

Another essential component is the **duration of the contract**, which must be no less than **twelve months**, unless there are valid reasons for derogation. Exceptions to the minimum term may apply, for instance, in the case of **seasonal products**, **one-off transactions**, or where the contract is concluded with the assistance of representative trade organisations for both parties. These exceptions reflect the legislator's intention to balance formal protection with practical flexibility.

The provisions concerning **price determination** are particularly significant. The price may either be set ex ante or made **determinable through objective and verifiable criteria**, such as weekly price listings published by the Chambers of Commerce, ISMEA data, or specific quality parameters. In certain cases—such as ornamental plants—even morphological features like **stem height** may serve as legitimate price indicators. The use of indeterminate or symbolic pricing structures is not permitted.

The contract must also specify the **terms of delivery**, including whether the goods are to be delivered to the buyer's premises, the seller's facility, or a third location, as well as the allocation of **transportation costs**.

With regard to **payment terms**, the law stipulates a **maximum period of thirty days** for perishable products and **sixty days** for non-perishable goods. These periods begin to run from the later of either the date of delivery or the moment when the price is definitively determined. In the case of **recurrent or staggered**

deliveries, the deadline runs from the final delivery—provided this occurs within one month—or from the determination of the price, whichever is later.

Lastly, the contract must include a **force majeure clause**, aimed at regulating the legal effects of unforeseeable, unavoidable events that are beyond the control of the parties and that materially disrupt the contractual balance. The inclusion of such a clause serves to uphold, to the greatest extent possible, the continuity of the contract, favouring **adaptation or renegotiation** rather than automatic termination.

4. The Sale of Grapes and Must in Light of the General Legal Framework and Its Sector-Specific Features

Grapes intended for winemaking fully qualify as agricultural products under both **European Union and Italian law**. Consequently, their sale for consideration—whether to industrial, commercial, or cooperative purchasers, or to other agricultural producers—**falls squarely within the scope of Legislative Decree No. 198/2021**, as subsequently amended. However, this set of rules operates within a **multilevel regulatory framework**, in which the domestic regulation of unfair trading practices must be **coordinated with sector-specific EU legislation**, in particular with the provisions governing the **Common Market Organisation (CMO) in the wine sector**.

In this context, particular importance is attached to the **rules on payment terms**, which may be subject to derogation from the ordinary regime under a **strictly defined set of conditions**. Derogation is permitted only where the contract concerns the **sale of grapes or must for the production of wine** and where **both** of the following conditions are met: first, the sale must take place within the context of a **multiannual contract**, or at least a contract that is expressly intended to become such; second, the clauses governing payment terms must be contained in **binding standard contracts** approved pursuant to **Article 164 of Regulation (EU) No. 1308/2013**, concluded prior to 1 January 2019, and **renewed after that date without materially worsening the supplier's position**.

Where even one of these two conditions is not met, the **mandatory payment terms** set out in the legislative decree shall apply in full: **thirty days** for **perishable products** (which fresh grapes typically are), and **sixty days** for non-perishable goods. In line with the general framework, the term shall run from the date of delivery or, where later, from the date on which the price is determined. In the case of recurrent or periodic deliveries, the term shall run from the **last**

delivery made (not exceeding one month) or, if later, from the determination of the price.

Beyond payment timing, a further aspect of particular relevance relates to **price determination**, which has been significantly affected by the innovations introduced by **Article 4 of Decree-Law No. 63 of 15 May 2024** (the so-called "Decreto Agricoltura"). This provision imposes a mandatory obligation to **take into account the supplier's production costs**, as well as the **average production cost** as determined by **ISMEA** (the Institute for Agricultural and Food Market Services). ISMEA is tasked with developing an **objective methodology for cost assessment**, to be submitted to the Ministry of Agriculture, and must regularly publish updated data on the average cost of producing grapes and must, reflecting the **prevailing technical conditions** across different regional contexts.

While not establishing a fixed price floor, compliance with such benchmarks introduces a **minimum threshold of economic legitimacy** for the price agreed upon by the parties, effectively ruling out contractual practices whereby the consideration is **manifestly below the producer's incurred costs**. This innovation is likely to have a **significant impact on grape supply contracts**, especially in market settings where **buyers wield disproportionate bargaining power**.

Finally, the regulatory structure is further reinforced by a provision—set out in **Article 3-bis of the same Decree-Law**—that establishes an **interconnection between national wine databases**. Specifically, the provision mandates the integration of the **electronic wine register** (which tracks inputs and outputs of wine products) with the **vineyard register**, which contains information on national wine-growing potential. This **data interoperability** is designed to improve transparency and traceability within the supply chain, with direct implications for the **verifiability of contractual flows** and the accuracy of data relating to grapes delivered or sold.

5. The Amendments Introduced by Decree-Law No. 63/2024 on Unfair Trading Practices

Decree-Law No. 63 of 15 May 2024, known as the "Decreto Agricoltura", introduced significant amendments and integrations to the regulatory framework established by Legislative Decree No. 198/2021, intervening on three major fronts: **price determination** in supply contracts, the **sanctioning regime**, and the **traceability system** for wine sector products.

The first and perhaps most consequential innovation is found in **Article 4** of the decree, which introduces the legal definitions of **"average production cost"** and **"production cost"**—concepts previously absent from national legislation on unfair trading practices but already present in institutional and technical debate at the EU level.

The **average production cost** is defined as the mean value, calculated by **ISMEA**, of the cost required to produce specific categories of agricultural and food products. This is to be determined using an objective assessment method developed by ISMEA itself and communicated to the Ministry of Agriculture. The rationale for introducing such a benchmark lies in the need to provide a **technical-institutional reference point** for price-setting, thereby **reinforcing protection for the weaker contractual party**—namely, the agricultural producer—and ensuring a **minimum level of remuneration**, in line with the objectives of **Article 39 TFEU**.

In parallel, the decree introduces the more concrete and operational notion of **production cost**, referring to the **actual expenses incurred** by an individual agricultural undertaking to produce a given good. This includes the use of **productive factors**—such as raw materials, labour, services, and amortisations—and reflects the specific agricultural techniques predominant in the relevant geographic area. Under the decree, this cost parameter forms the basis on which the parties must negotiate the price in supply contracts. While not constituting a rigid price floor, this provision sets a **non-derogable lower threshold**, thereby excluding the legitimacy of contractual agreements where the price falls below the supplier's actual production costs. Violations of this principle may expose the buyer to **administrative sanctions**, and in more serious cases, **contract nullity**.

The second area of reform concerns the **sanctions regime**, which has been partially revised to include **deflationary mechanisms**. Article 4 of the decree introduces a **remedial incentive scheme**, under which a non-compliant operator, following an inspection by the **ICQRF** (Central Inspectorate for the Protection of Quality and Fraud Repression of Agri-Food Products), may benefit from a **50% reduction of the applicable sanction**, provided they can demonstrate having adopted corrective measures capable of neutralising the effects of the infringement. Such measures may include the formalisation in writing of a previously oral contract or the **revision of onerous contractual terms** initially imposed unilaterally, including by offering the supplier a price that aligns with their production costs.

This provision, inspired by principles of **proportionality and reasonableness**, aims to balance the **deterrent function of administrative penalties** with a restorative approach, incentivising **compliance-oriented behaviour** and reducing litigation. From this perspective, it represents an important evolution of the system, shifting the emphasis from the mere formal finding of an infraction to the **effective remediation of the harm** suffered by the supplier.

Finally, as already noted, **Decree-Law No. 63/2024** provides for a significant advancement in the **traceability and transparency of commercial flows in the wine sector**. Article 3-bis introduces a **functional interconnection between the electronic wine register**—which records data on the intake and outflow of wine products—and the **vineyard register**, which contains updated information on winegrowing potential. This interoperability will **enhance controls** over the origin, movement, and destination of wine products, offering valuable tools for verifying the **consistency between declared data and contractual terms**. It thus constitutes a complementary but structurally significant step in building a **more equitable, regulated, and resilient supply chain**.

6. The Critical Tension Between Contractual Freedom and Regulatory Constraints in Price Determination

The **determination of price** in contracts for the sale of agricultural and food products represents, from a systematic standpoint, one of the areas where the **tension between the principle of contractual autonomy** (Article 1322 of the Italian Civil Code) and the **need for public regulation to safeguard fairness** in commercial relationships is most evident. The **obligation introduced by Decree-Law No. 63/2024** to take into account both the **production costs borne by the supplier** and the **average production cost established by ISMEA**—although not amounting to an authoritative price fixing—nonetheless entails a **significant limitation on the parties' contractual discretion**, particularly in supply chains marked by substantial asymmetries in economic power.

From the perspective of **contract law**, the requirement to anchor price determination—even by mere reference—to an actual cost undermines the traditional principle that the consideration in a contract may be freely agreed upon by the parties. In practice, especially within fragmented and poorly organised agricultural sectors, pricing has long reflected not the economic sustainability of production, but rather the urgency to place the product on the market and the relative bargaining strength of the supplier.

This regulatory innovation seeks to **correct such imbalances**, yet it raises legitimate concerns regarding its **compatibility with EU law**, particularly with the principle of **free competition** and the **prohibition of minimum price setting**, as interpreted on several occasions by the Court of Justice of the European Union. While it is true that **Directive (EU) 2019/633** allows Member States to adopt protective measures beyond the harmonised minimum, such measures must still be **proportionate, non-discriminatory**, and **justified by overriding public interests**, such as the protection of agricultural labour dignity or the preservation of rural environments.

From a practical standpoint, the establishment of a **de facto minimum price**—based on standardised parameters such as those provided by ISMEA—may lead to **interpretative disputes and litigation**, especially in cases where the contractually agreed price diverges significantly from the statistical benchmark. This scenario raises several issues: the burden of proof regarding actual production costs, the reliability of public data, and the **territorial and sectoral variability of production costs**.

Indeed, agricultural production conditions are **highly heterogeneous**: one need only consider differences in labour costs between northern and southern Italy, variations in production methods (conventional, organic, integrated), or disparities in fixed costs depending on farm size. A single "average price" may, in such cases, **unintentionally penalise certain operators while favouring others**, thereby producing internal market distortions rather than correcting them.

From a legal standpoint, this calls for a **careful balancing** between the goal of ensuring **fair remuneration for producers**—consistent with **Article 39 TFEU** and **Article 9 of the Italian Constitution**, which protects the rural and agro-environmental heritage—and the need to **avoid unduly constraining contractual freedom**, particularly within a single market framework.

In this sense, the obligation to consider production costs should not be read as a **rigid and insurmountable constraint**, but rather as a **standard for assessing the fairness of buyer conduct**, including for the purposes of establishing the existence of an unfair trading practice. Accordingly, the rule serves both a **preventive function**, by discouraging excessively low and abusive pricing arrangements, and a **sanctioning function**, where the agreed price is clearly disproportionate to the documented production costs.

7. Sanctions, Remedial Mechanisms, and the Impact on Supply Chain Organisation

The **sanctions regime introduced by Legislative Decree No. 198/2021** has been revised by **Decree-Law No. 63/2024**, which adopts a more selective approach to enforcement by combining **enhanced administrative controls** with **dispute-reducing measures** and incentives for **voluntary regularisation** by non-compliant operators. The legislative rationale is to move away from a strictly punitive model in favour of a **responsible enforcement framework**, focused on the swift remediation of the harm caused by unfair practices, without necessarily resorting to the full imposition of monetary penalties.

Specifically, the new mechanism provides that, **in the event of a violation detected following an inspection by the ICQRF** (Central Inspectorate for the Protection of Quality and Fraud Repression of Agri-Food Products), the infringing party may benefit from a **50% reduction in the administrative fine**, provided they can demonstrate having taken **corrective actions capable of neutralising the effects of the offence**.

The decree offers examples of eligible remedial conduct, including: the **formalisation of a contract initially concluded orally**; the **modification of contractual terms unilaterally imposed by the buyer**; or the **revision of the agreed price** to bring it in line with the **supplier's actual production costs**, where the original consideration was manifestly disproportionate.

Although introduced as a simplification measure, this provision carries **broader systemic significance**. First, it gives legal weight to **post-delictum behaviour** by the transgressor, thereby encouraging voluntary compliance. Second, it acknowledges that agricultural contracts serve not only a **commutative function**, but also a **social and solidaristic role**, where the correction of contractual imbalance is valuable in itself, regardless of the penalty imposed.

From an operational standpoint, access to the reduced sanction regime **depends on a discretionary assessment by the competent authority**, which must determine whether the corrective measures adopted are truly effective in rebalancing the contractual relationship. This is not a mechanistic evaluation but one that requires **case-by-case scrutiny**, taking into account factors such as the **good faith** of the offender, the **timeliness** of the remedial action, and the **absence or presence of repeated infractions**.

Moreover, the revised regime is embedded in an administrative landscape that increasingly relies on **digital monitoring tools and supply chain traceability**, facilitated by the **interconnection between telematic registers and sectoral databases**. This strengthening of ex ante control mechanisms serves to reduce the risk of systemic violations and, at least in the long term, promotes a **contractual model based more on proactive compliance** than reactive sanctioning.

Lastly, one must not overlook the **indirect structural effects** that the reform may have on the organisation of supply chain relationships. The **increased informational and formal obligations** imposed on purchasing enterprises could lead to a **selective filtration of suppliers**, favouring those with greater contractual reliability and better documentation of production costs. This dynamic may **enhance the role of producer organisations and cooperatives**, which are better equipped—both technically and legally—to manage compliant contracts, but may also result in the **marginalisation of smaller agricultural operators**, who lack the resources to meet such procedural demands.

In this light, the rationalisation of the sanctions regime is not merely a tool of repression, but rather a form of **regulatory engineering** aimed at reshaping supply chain contracting practices into **fairer, more structured, and more transparent arrangements**, in line with the objectives set out in **Directive (EU) 2019/633** and the principles underlying the **Single CMO Regulation.**

8. Critical Reflections and Systemic Perspectives

The strengthening of the regulatory framework on unfair trading practices through **Legislative Decree No. 198/2021**, as supplemented by **Decree-Law No. 63/2024**, reflects an increasing institutional commitment to constructing **more balanced and structurally transparent contractual relationships** within the agri-food supply chain. Nevertheless, this legislative evolution gives rise to **a number of critical questions**, both regarding the **practical effectiveness of the protections** afforded and the **consistency of the new regime** with market principles and the **peculiarities of individual production sectors**.

A first concern lies in the risk of **regulatory homogenisation**: the extension of a **single legal framework to all contractual relationships** within the agri-food chain—including transactions between farmers or between members and their cooperatives—risks **flattening the structural and functional diversity** that characterises the various forms of economic organisation within the primary sector. Consider, for instance, the wine sector, where contractual relationships between growers and cooperative wineries are often governed by **mutualistic**

logics, which may not be easily reconcilable with the rigidity of rules designed for strictly commercial transactions.

A second critical issue concerns the **impact of linking price determination to production costs** on the broader mechanisms of value creation. While the aim is to prevent **abusive practices and symbolic remuneration**, the introduction of an **institutional benchmark**—such as the ISMEA average production cost—may inadvertently **freeze contractual dynamics** and hinder the **valorisation of premium or niche products**, whose price reflects not merely input costs but also **perceived quality, brand identity**, and **market positioning strategies**. In the absence of sufficiently flexible adjustment criteria, there is a tangible risk that a public benchmark may operate as a **de facto price ceiling**, generating distortions especially for operators in the **high-end market segments**.

Further concerns arise from the **administrative and operational burden** imposed by the new rules. The obligation to formalise contracts in writing and maintain detailed documentation—although justifiable in terms of legal certainty—can prove a **significant obstacle for small agricultural enterprises**, which form the backbone of the Italian agri-food economy but often operate with **limited managerial capacity**. The widespread adoption of complex contractual models could result in **uneven access to regulatory compliance**, disadvantaging less structured operators and accelerating **market consolidation** in favour of larger, more organised entities.

Finally, at the European level, one cannot overlook the fact that the **indirect imposition of minimum pricing thresholds**, even in parametric form, could raise **compatibility issues with EU competition law**, especially if the national mechanism is perceived as a form of **disguised protectionism**. For this reason, the **dialogue between Italian domestic regulation and the EU legal framework** will be crucial going forward—both at the **interpretative level** (in judicial settings) and at the **regulatory level** (e.g., through notification and evaluation procedures under **Article 114 TFEU**).

In conclusion, although the regulatory framework on unfair trading practices addresses widely shared concerns about contractual imbalances, it also compels a broader rethinking of the role of the agricultural contract in the contemporary era. Such contracts can no longer be regarded as mere instruments of exchange between formally equal parties, but rather as points of convergence between private autonomy and public objectives in the field of agricultural and food policy—an equilibrium that remains very much a work in progress.

The Regulation of the Wine Sector under the 2023–2027 CAP: Legal Instruments, Strategic Objectives, and Operational Impacts

Fracesco Tedioli
*** Agricultural Law Expert Attorney, independent arbitrator and Adjunct Professor of Commercial law at the University of Mantova (Italy).**

Table of Contents:

1. Continuity and Change in Support for the Wine Sector

The wine sector has always held a strategic position within the agricultural landscape of the European Union, not only due to the high economic value of its production and exports but also for its identity-related and territorial significance. Under the framework of the Common Agricultural Policy (CAP) 2023–2027, this sector continues to benefit from a differentiated treatment, based on a combination of sectoral measures, horizontal instruments, and market rules, reflecting the EU's intent to balance production stability with environmental objectives and competitiveness.

The current legal framework of the CAP is defined, in general terms, by Regulation (EU) 2021/2115, which establishes the CAP Strategic Plans, and by Regulation (EU) 2021/2117, which amends the rules governing the Common Market Organisation (CMO) set out in Regulation (EU) No. 1308/2013. It is this latter regulation that reaffirms—albeit with significant additions—the legal architecture of the sectoral support for wine, thereby underscoring the necessity to ensure an autonomous and structured regime tailored to the technical, economic, and environmental specificities of European viticulture.

Compared to the 2014–2022 programming period, the new CAP preserves many of the core principles underlying wine support, but embeds them within a system that emphasises the strategic and contractual nature of interventions, granting Member States broad margins for programming. The result is a highly differentiated approach, where wine support is no longer implemented through a rigidly vertical logic but is instead framed within a National Strategic Plan (NSP) that must integrate environmental, social, and income-related considerations, while maintaining consistency with EU competition law and the broader objectives of the European Green Deal.

The retention of a dedicated sectoral programme for wine, complete with a specific financial allocation, confirms the EU institutions' recognition of the need to maintain tailor-made tools for high-value-added sectors with strong exposure to international markets. At the same time, the strengthening of environmental conditionality, the promotion of innovation, and the alignment with rural development goals have led to a rebalancing between direct payments, sectoral interventions, and structural investments.

In this evolving context, the wine sector remains one of the few agricultural sectors in Europe to benefit from a long-standing sector-specific support scheme. Nevertheless, it is increasingly called upon to engage with horizontal integration, requiring a reorganisation of business strategies, cooperative models, and supply chain dynamics, in full alignment with the new paradigms that underpin the current CAP.

2. Direct Payments in the 2023–2027 CAP: A Marginal Yet Non-Negligible Role for Viticulture

Within the overall framework of the CAP 2023–2027, direct payments represent the principal tool for supporting farmers' income and ensuring a basic economic safety net. However, the wine sector—historically excluded from the single payment scheme introduced by the Fischler reform of 2003—continues to play only a marginal role in this regard, benefiting solely in an indirect manner from the resources allocated through payment entitlements.

The rationale behind this exclusion is structural: it lies in the high level of competitiveness and market orientation characterising the wine sector, which led EU legislators to favour sector-specific intervention mechanisms over a generalised income support model. Nevertheless, certain winegrowers—especially those managing mixed farms or those who historically received aid entitlements on vineyard areas before the 2008 reform—may still be beneficiaries of direct payments under the current programming period, depending on eligibility criteria and the ownership of valid CAP entitlements.

In the new architecture of direct payments set out under Regulation (EU) 2021/2115, particular emphasis is placed on the concept of enhanced conditionality, which integrates statutory management requirements and standards of good agricultural and environmental condition (GAEC), extending them to all farmed areas, including vineyards. Thus, although not formally targeted by income support measures, the wine sector is still subject to a form of indirect regulatory conditioning, which shapes its agronomic practices and management decisions.

Another point of intersection between direct payments and the viticultural sector lies in redistributive and inclusive interventions, such as support for young farmers and redistributive payments for small and medium-sized holdings. These measures may potentially benefit wine producers, provided that they meet the eligibility thresholds. However, their actual impact on the income of wine farms remains limited and is heavily influenced by national implementation choices and by the structural characteristics of Italian viticulture, which is marked by a strong prevalence of specialised, market-oriented enterprises, often ineligible for size-based preferential schemes.

It is also important to stress that the marginal role of direct payments for the wine sector does not imply a diminished relevance of the sector within the CAP as a whole. Rather, it reflects a functional differentiation of policy instruments, in line with the principle of subsidiarity and the strategic autonomy granted to Member States in the design of their national plans. Within this framework, viticulture remains a highly regulated sector, governed by a combination of sectoral, environmental, market, and rural development measures that extend well beyond the scope of direct income support.

3. Eco-Schemes and Environmental Sustainability: Selective Opportunities for Winegrowers

One of the most significant innovations introduced by the 2023–2027 CAP is the implementation of eco-schemes, annual payment instruments aimed at incentivising farming practices that deliver environmental or climatic benefits exceeding the baseline standards of conditionality. These measures, provided for in Article 31 of Regulation (EU) 2021/2115, fall within the scope of the CAP's first pillar but are conceptually aligned with rural development policies, combining environmental objectives with income support conditional upon the adoption of sustainable practices.

For the wine sector, access to eco-schemes constitutes a potential—but not universal—opportunity. Their application is subject to a dual filtering mechanism: on the one hand, the willingness of the Member State to include viticulture-compatible measures within its National Strategic Plan (NSP); on the other, the actual capacity of winegrowers to adapt their farming practices to the eligibility requirements.

In the Italian case, the NSP outlines five eco-schemes, two of which are potentially applicable to vineyards: payments for the increase of permanent green cover and payments for adherence to integrated or organic production systems. Both measures may be relevant for viticulture, but only insofar as wine producers formally adopt and document compatible practices—such as inter-row grassing, reduction in pesticide use, or compliance with regional certification protocols.

However, the implementation of eco-schemes in the wine sector presents numerous operational challenges. First, the physical layout of vineyards—with permanent rows and mechanised soil management—limits the uniform applicability of grass cover, especially in hilly or sloped areas. Second, the costs associated with adapting practices and obtaining certification may act as a deterrent for small and medium-sized enterprises, particularly where the economic benefits do not substantially outweigh the compliance costs already incurred under ordinary environmental regulations.

As such, participation in eco-schemes requires a case-by-case technical and economic assessment, taking into account both agronomic compatibility and the financial sustainability of the commitment. This dynamic tends to create a polarisation between structurally robust enterprises—capable of leveraging eco-scheme opportunities through internal resources or specialised consultancy—and more marginal operators, who may be excluded from these schemes due to organisational or informational barriers.

From a legal standpoint, eco-schemes represent a hybrid regulatory instrument, combining mandatory and voluntary components: Member States are required to allocate at least 25% of their direct payments to these schemes, yet farmer participation remains voluntary. For the wine sector, this means that eco-schemes do not constitute a structural support mechanism, but rather a selective opportunity whose impact depends on the coherence between planning objectives, implementation tools, and the operators' ability to capture the associated benefits

4. Sectoral Support for Wine: Objectives, Beneficiaries, and Legal Framework

The wine sector is one of the few agricultural supply chains in Europe for which the Union has retained, even under the 2023–2027 CAP, a specific and structured sectoral support regime, governed within the framework of the Common Market Organisation (CMO). This regime is legally based on Articles 58 to 60 of Regulation (EU) 2021/2117, which amends Regulation (EU) No. 1308/2013, confirming the strategic approach already tested in previous programming periods.

Sectoral support for wine does not take the form of a generic intervention, but rather of a structured programme of eligible measures, defined and implemented by the Member States through specific multiannual national support programmes, subject to approval by the European Commission. In Italy, the operational reference is the National Support Programme for the Wine Sector (PNS Vino), implemented in accordance with EU guidelines, but adapted to the territorial and production specificities of the national context.

The portfolio of eligible measures includes interventions designed to support the competitiveness, sustainability, and commercial promotion of wine products. These include, in particular:

- restructuring and conversion of vineyards, aimed at improving quality, varietal adaptation, and production efficiency;
- investments in tangible and intangible assets, including winemaking and processing technologies;
- promotion measures in third countries, which are strategic for supporting internationalisation;
- information campaigns on responsible consumption and the geographical origin of wines;
- crisis management tools, such as crop insurance, green harvesting aid, and crisis distillation schemes.

The financial resources allocated to Italy under the PNS Vino are determined on an annual basis and distributed among the regions according to criteria agreed upon within the State-Regions Conference. National co-financing and private cost-sharing make the programme a highly efficient tool for resource allocation, capable of stimulating targeted investments and mobilising additional funds at the local level.

From a legal perspective, the distinctive feature of sectoral wine support lies in its programmed and contractual nature. Each measure may be activated only following the submission of an application responding to regional calls for proposals, which is a prerequisite for accessing the support. Applications are evaluated on the basis of pre-established priority criteria, with technical assessments that consider the economic, environmental, and social impact of the proposed investments. This procedural structure ensures a high degree of selectivity and transparency, but at the same time requires significant organisational capacity on the part of the beneficiaries, who must demonstrate sound management, solvency, and project planning skills.

The purpose of sectoral support is not to replace the market, but rather to facilitate the structural adjustment of the wine sector, encouraging its transition towards more resilient, competitive, and sustainable production models. It therefore constitutes a strategic instrument, particularly relevant in a context of increasing environmental pressure, market volatility, and shifting consumer preferences.

Finally, it is important to emphasise that the wine sector support regime is fully compatible with EU State aid rules, as it is established under general Union law and implemented through ex ante authorised procedures. This ensures that public support does not distort internal or international trade, and that producers across Member States benefit from a level playing field in terms of legal protection and market access.

5. Authorisations for Vine Planting: Current Regime and Reform Perspectives

Among the structural regulatory tools applicable to the wine sector, the system of authorisations for vine planting represents one of the most significant instruments from a legal, economic, and policy standpoint. Introduced by Regulation (EU) No. 1308/2013 as a replacement for the former planting rights regime, this system was extended until 2045 by Regulation (EU) 2021/2117, with a mid-term review scheduled for 2028 to assess its effectiveness and alignment with the general objectives of the CAP.

The rationale underpinning the authorisation regime lies in the need to prevent market imbalances resulting from uncontrolled expansion of vineyard surfaces, while simultaneously preserving the quality, reputation, and sustainability of European wine production. In essence, it is a system of ex ante planning, allowing Member States to selectively manage the growth of production potential by granting free but conditional authorisations.

In Italy, the regime is governed by the Ministerial Decree of 30 November 2015, implementing the EU legislation and supplemented by regional provisions. The system establishes three types of authorisations:

- New plantings, granted annually in an amount not exceeding 1% of the national planted vineyard area;
- Replanting following the grubbing-up of vineyards, to be exercised within six years;
- Conversion of rights acquired prior to 2015 into authorisations valid until 2025.

Authorisations are issued following the assessment of applications submitted at the regional level, according to priority criteria established at the national level, in line with the principles set out in Article 64 of Regulation (EU) No. 1308/2013. These criteria include intended use for protected designations of origin (PDOs) or protected geographical indications (PGIs), support for young farmers and small businesses, location in areas of high environmental or landscape value, and compliance with sustainable production systems.

From a legal perspective, planting authorisations do not constitute full subjective rights, but rather administrative entitlements subject to temporal and functional constraints. Failure to utilise the authorisation within the specified period leads to its expiration and may trigger administrative penalties. Compliance with the declared use and with the priority criteria is therefore of substantial importance, including for the purposes of ex post controls by the competent administrative authority.

The practical implementation of the authorisation regime has, however, revealed a number of operational shortcomings and interpretative tensions. In particular, the management of demand exceeding the available area has led to litigation, allegations of circumvention through fictitious leases, and concerns over transparency in the selection of applications. The adoption of centralised digital tools and the ongoing integration with the vineyard register and the wine e-register are important rationalisation measures, but they do not obviate the need for a systemic reform aimed at improving efficiency, traceability, and consistency with the objectives of quality and sustainability.

Looking ahead, any reform of the authorisation regime must address the delicate balance between entrepreneurial freedom, planning requirements, and protection of designations, in a context shaped by international competition and climate change. Such reform should promote greater flexibility without undermining the strategic importance of controlling production potential. In this framework, the legal nature of authorisations should be reaffirmed as a crucial regulatory safeguard, to be strengthened through more uniform interpretation and clearer accountability of the competent authorities.

6. Towards an Integrated and Differentiated Wine Policy

An analysis of the Common Agricultural Policy (CAP) 2023–2027 through the lens of the wine sector reveals a complex regulatory model, articulated on distinct yet interdependent levels: on the one hand, a consolidated sectoral support framework, which remains the principal instrument of public intervention; on the other, the gradual integration of viticulture into environmental, redistributive, and developmental strategies that cut across the CAP as a whole.

Viticulture thus stands at the intersection of regulatory specificity and programmatic horizontality: while it continues to benefit from exclusive measures—such as planting authorisations and national support programmes—it is increasingly required to comply with overarching principles and objectives, such as environmental sustainability, economic resilience, and territorial cohesion. This legal evolution reflects a shift in paradigm: the sector is no longer governed through a protective lens, but rather valorised within a framework of integrated and multi-level governance.

From a strictly legal perspective, this transition implies a growing importance of selective procedures, planning instruments, and control mechanisms, which now constitute core components of eligibility for public support. Entitlement to aid no longer derives merely from possessing vineyard surfaces or compliant production, but from the operator's ability to engage with strategies aligned with the objectives of the National Strategic Plan, to comply with increasingly stringent environmental and social requirements, and to demonstrate the public utility of the proposed intervention.

This evolution calls for a renewed reflection on the role of agricultural law, which is increasingly tasked not only with regulating economic relationships but also with interpreting constitutional and EU principles on sustainability, land protection, and social justice. In this sense, the legal framework applicable to the wine sector acquires a normative and ordering function, capable of guiding productive choices, shaping collective behaviour, and promoting institutional and interprofessional cooperation.

Ultimately, the wine sector—due to its economic importance, organisational sophistication, and deep territorial embeddedness—emerges as an advanced legal and administrative laboratory within the CAP. The challenge for the near future will be to reconcile this normative richness with the need for simplification, fairness, and adaptability, thereby ensuring a European wine policy that is at once integrated, differentiated, and dynamically oriented towards the common good.

The Concept of "Connected Activities" in the Wine Sector under Italian Agricultural Law

By Vanni Fusconi, Lawyer

Summary

1. From Agricultural Practice to Prevalence: The Evolution of Article 2135 and Its Impact on Winegrowers

The Italian Law on Agricultural Orientation (***Legge di orientamento in agricoltura***), formally titled "Orientation and Modernisation of the Agricultural Sector", introduced a substantial revision of Article 2135 of the Civil Code, redefining the legal boundaries of agricultural activities and, in particular, of connected agricultural activities (***attività agricole connesse***).

The new legislative framework marked a decisive shift away from the outdated notion of "normal agricultural practice"[54] and introduced the more flexible and economically oriented criterion of prevalence. This change has important implications: it reduces the centrality of the land as the defining element of agricultural activity, and recognises instead that agriculture may be carried out with increasing organisational complexity and investment capacity[55], as long as the connection between the ancillary and the core agricultural activity is preserved under the criterion of prevalence[56].

The guiding principles of the 2001 reform find their most complete application in the wine sector, which more than any other reflects the evolution of agriculture into a structurally entrepreneurial field. Today's winegrower-entrepreneur is no longer limited to the primary production of grapes but invests in the development and growth of the business—through processing of grapes into wine, product manipulation (such as blending), branding, and continuous innovation aimed at expanding product lines and market positioning.

---

54 By "normality" was meant what most farmers customarily did—that is, what a farmer would ordinarily do in a given area (*Cass. S.U., 10 October 1955, No. 2451*). From a legal standpoint, the concept of "normality" was thus more accurately framed as "typicality." What is normal is what is typical in the organisation of the agricultural enterprise—not what the entrepreneur arbitrarily decides to do. Cf. G. Galloni, ***Lezioni** sul diritto dell'impresa agricola*, Naples, 1980, p. 195.

55 "*La natura agricola non è esclusa dall'esistenza di rilevanti parametri di natura quantitativa, non più incompatibili con la nuova formulazione dell'art. 2135 c.c., onde la dimensione dell'impresa, la complessità della organizzazione, la consistenza degli investimenti e l'ampiezza del volume d'affari non sono di per sé automaticamente incompatibili con la natura solo agricola dell'impresa*" (Cass. 10 dicembre 2010, n. 24995; Cass. 16 gennaio 2018, n. 831).

56 "*This amendment must be interpreted as reflecting the legislator's intention to move beyond a purely "land-based" conception of agriculture—one founded exclusively on the centrality of the territorial element—and to replace it with a more dynamic approach, consistent with the evolving technical and economic reality, in which productive structures that use land as a supporting instrument assume a dominant role*". (***Italian Supreme Court, Civil Section I, 10 December 2010, No. 24995***)

In this process of growth and diversification, however, agricultural enterprises must comply with the criterion of "prevalence", as clearly stated in paragraph 3 of Article 2135 of the Italian Civil Code[57], in order to maintain their legal classification as agricultural businesses and benefit from the associated legal and tax regimes.

2. The Requirement of Connection in Wine Production

2.1 Fiscal Recognition of Connected Activities

From a fiscal perspective, the notion of connected activities in wine production is codified in Article 32, paragraph 2, letter c) of the Italian Consolidated Income Tax Act (TUIR – D.P.R. No. 917 of 22 December 1986), as amended by Article 2, paragraph 6, letter a) of Law No. 350 of 24 December 2003.

According to this provision, certain activities—specifically, the handling, preservation, processing, marketing, and valorisation of agricultural products—may fall under the category of agricultural income (*reddito agrario*), provided that:

- The activities concern products explicitly listed in a ministerial decree;
- The products are obtained predominantly through the cultivation of land, forestry, or animal husbandry by the agricultural entrepreneur.

This framework extends the definition of agricultural activity to include certain post-harvest operations, but only when these are applied to products primarily derived from the entrepreneur's own agricultural activity.

57 Article 2135 of the Italian Civil Code – Agricultural Entrepreneur An agricultural entrepreneur is a person who engages in one or more of the following activities: cultivation of land, forestry, animal husbandry, and connected activities. For the purposes of this article, cultivation of land, forestry, and animal husbandry refer to activities aimed at the care and development of a biological cycle—or of a necessary phase thereof—of a vegetal or animal nature, which make use of, or are capable of making use of, land, woodland, or inland, brackish, or marine waters. Connected activities shall in any case include those carried out by the same agricultural entrepreneur that are directed at the handling, preservation, processing, marketing, and valorisation of products predominantly obtained from the cultivation of land, forestry, or animal husbandry. Also considered connected are those activities that provide goods or services, through the prevalent use of equipment or resources of the agricultural holding normally employed in the agricultural activity carried out, including activities aimed at the valorisation of the territory and of the rural and forestry heritage, as well as reception and hospitality services, as defined by law.

2.2 The Legislative Use of Sequential Terminology and Interpretive Issues

The use of a sequential list of verbs—***manipolazione, conservazione, trasformazione, commercializzazione, valorizzazione*** (handling, preservation, processing, marketing, and valorisation)—has led to interpretative uncertainty. On a literal reading, one might assume that even performing only one of these activities could suffice to qualify as an agricultural connected activity.

However, the Italian Revenue Agency (*Agenzia delle Entrate*)[58], aligning with consistent case law from the Court of Cassation, has clarified that mere commercialisation or preservation, in isolation, cannot qualify as connected activities for tax purposes. Instead, a substantial element of "manipulation" or "transformation" is necessary to meet the legal definition[59][60].

This interpretation is confirmed in the explanatory report accompanying the Ministerial Decree of 19 March 2004, which lists the eligible agricultural products. The report states that those five activities, if performed individually, do not produce agricultural income under Article 32(2)(c) TUIR[61], but rather

58 In order to provide an exhaustive definition of the concepts of ***"transformation"*** and ***"manipulation"*** in the agricultural and agro-industrial sectors, reference must be made to the clarifications issued by the Italian Ministry in Circular No. 351690 of 1955, which states: 1) Manipulation: a product is considered to have been manipulated when, despite undergoing certain forms of processing, it retains its original commercial characteristics. Typical examples include sorting, drying, and packaging of tobacco leaves. 2) Transformation: transformation is understood as an industrial process through which one product is converted into another that is commercially different. The product resulting from the transformation must be assigned a different customs classification code than that of the original material.

59 *Italian Supreme Court (Corte di Cassazione), Civil Section*, Judgment No. 18488 of 13 September 2004, Judgment No. 7238 of 13 April 2015, Judgment No. 18828 of 28 July 2017.

60 *It is appropriate to clarify that transformation occurs when, as a result of processing, the original product loses the commercial characteristics that previously defined it—for instance, cereals used to produce flour or olives processed to obtain oil. By contrast, manipulation occurs when the product, despite the processing it undergoes, retains its original commercial identity, as in the case of cleaning and packaging vegetables or fruit.* (***Italian Supreme Court, Judgment No. 8128 of 21 April 2016***)

61 Article 32 of the Italian Consolidated Income Tax Act (TUIR) – Agricultural Income. Agricultural income consists of the portion of the average ordinary income of land attributable to the capital employed and the organisational labour used, within the limits of the productive capacity of the land, in carrying out agricultural activities thereon. The following are considered agricultural activities: a) activities directed at the cultivation of land and forestry; b) animal husbandry, provided that at least one quarter of the feed is obtainable from the land, and activities directed at the production of plants using fixed or mobile, including temporary, structures, as long as the production area does not exceed twice the size of the land on which the production itself takes place; c) the activities referred to in the third paragraph of Article 2135 of the Civil Code, consisting in the handling, preservation, processing, marketing, and valorisation—even if not carried out on the land—of products predominantly obtained from the cultivation of the land, forestry, or animal husbandry, with reference to the goods

generate business income (***reddito d'impresa***) subject to the rules of Article 55 TUIR.

2.3 Manipulation and Transformation in the Wine Sector

In the context of the wine sector, the concept of transformation is relatively uncontroversial, as wine is legally and commercially distinct from grapes. However, defining what constitutes "manipulation" is more complex.

The Revenue Agency has clarified that certain enological operations—such as the addition of preservatives for hygiene and health purposes, or filtration for microbiological stabilization—can be classified as manipulation.

Thus, the sale of wine purchased from third parties, provided it is not predominant and has been subjected to legitimate manipulation, may be included among connected agricultural activities[62].

2.4 Externalised Processing and the Principle of Prevalence

With the amendment of Article 32 TUIR by Law No. 350/2003, the old reference to activities conducted in accordance with "normal agricultural practice" was replaced by the criterion of prevalence and the specification of eligible goods. As a result, the new rules apply even where the processing stages are outsourced to third parties—for example, when a grower uses an external winery to process their own grapes.

This flexible interpretation is especially relevant in a sector like wine production, where shared facilities, processing consortia, and external vinification are common and economically efficient practices.

---

identified every two years, taking into account the criteria set forth in paragraph 1, by decree of the Minister of Economy and Finance, upon proposal of the Minister of Agricultural and Forestry Policies. By decree of the Minister of Finance, in agreement with the Minister of Agriculture and Forestry, the number of livestock per species that falls within the limits set out in letter b) of paragraph 2 shall be determined, taking into account the productive capacity of the land and the required forage units depending on the species being raised. Land referred to in Article 24, paragraph 2, shall not be considered as generating agricultural income.

62 In a clarification issued on 12 January 2009, the Italian Revenue Agency (Agenzia delle Entrate) specified that: "*Winemaking activities carried out by an agricultural entrepreneur using quantities of wine purchased from third parties, which are subsequently subjected to further processing within the farm before being placed on the market, fall within the scope of connected agricultural activities and generate agricultural income under Article 32 of the Consolidated Income Tax Act (TUIR), provided that the principle of prevalence is respected—meaning that the quantity of wine produced from the entrepreneur's own grapes must exceed that purchased from third parties.*

2.5 The Role of Ministerial Classifications in Determining Eligible Products

To ensure that a post-harvest activity—such as processing or manipulation—qualifies as a connected agricultural activity for tax purposes, it is not sufficient for the product to be of agricultural origin. It must also be explicitly listed in the ministerial decree that identifies which products are eligible under Article 32, paragraph 2, letter c) of the Italian Consolidated Income Tax Act (TUIR)[63].

In the context of wine production, this means that only the processing of grapes into wine (as opposed to other types of alcoholic beverages or food products) can fall under the favorable agricultural income regime, and only when the products involved are among those enumerated in the official list. Specifically, the decree includes the following ATECO activity codes:

- 01.21.0: Cultivation of grapes[64];
- 11.02.1 and 11.02.2: Production of wine and related beverages.

These codes identify both the primary agricultural production (grape growing) and the connected processing stages (vinification), thus forming a coherent regulatory chain that aligns with the principle of "prevalence" outlined in Article 2135 of the Civil Code.

In practice, this means that even if a winegrower engages in transformation or manipulation activities, these will only qualify as connected and remain within the agricultural tax regime if:

- The products processed are derived primarily from the farm's own production; and

63 Ministerial Decree of 13 February 2015, identifying the products to which the provisions of Article 32(2)(c) TUIR apply, pursuant to the proposal of the Ministry of Agricultural and Forestry Policies.

64 For manipulation and transformation activities involving products other than those listed in the Ministerial Decree—provided that the prevalence requirement is still respected—a lump-sum taxation regime has been introduced under Article 56-*bis*, paragraph 2 of the Consolidated Income Tax Act (TUIR). According to this regime, income is determined by applying a 15% coefficient to the amount of revenues recorded for value-added tax (VAT) purposes.

As clarified in Circular No. 44/E of 2004, this provision does not apply to transformation activities that: 1) Are not customarily carried out in the context of agricultural operations; 2) Take place at a stage subsequent to the original transformation that generated the products listed in the Ministerial Decree; 3) And result in entirely new products, which can no longer be regarded as connected to the main agricultural activity as defined by Article 2135 of the Italian Civil Code.

- The finished goods belong to one of the categories listed in the ministerial decree.

This regulatory system not only ensures consistency and legal certainty, but also prevents the extension of favorable tax treatment to activities that, although related to agriculture in a broad sense, fall outside the core of agricultural production and transformation as recognised by law.

3. The Prevalence Requirement in the Use of Third-Party Products

One of the most important conditions for classifying a processing or manipulation activity as "connected" under Italian agricultural law is the respect of the prevalence criterion, expressly laid down in Article 2135, paragraph 3 of the Civil Code and reiterated in Article 32 of the TUIR.

This principle states that, in order for the transformation or manipulation of products purchased from third parties to remain within the agricultural framework, the farm's own production must be quantitatively prevalent over the external inputs.

3.1 Enhancing Quality and Diversifying Production: When Third-Party Purchases Are Permitted

The law does not prohibit the use of third-party agricultural products altogether. On the contrary, their limited and strategic use is permitted—indeed, sometimes encouraged—when it serves to:

- Improve the quality of the final product (e.g., blending wine to enhance structure or aromatic profile);
- Expand the product range offered by the farm, provided that the newly introduced products fall within the same productive sector (e.g., viticulture, fruit growing, livestock)[65].

For instance, a wine producer who cultivates red grapes and decides to purchase a small quantity of white grapes in order to offer a white wine may remain within the legal framework of connected agricultural activity. Conversely, a winegrower who purchases milk to produce cheese would not meet the

---

65 The expansion of the product range (***aumento di gamma***) is permitted only insofar as it concerns goods belonging to the same agronomic sector. This principle has been affirmed by the Italian Revenue Agency in Circulars No. 44/E of 2002 and No. 44/E of 2004, and confirmed by the Italian Supreme Court in Judgment No. 18071 of 21 July 2017; Council of State (*Consiglio di Stato*), Judgment No. 4441 of 18 July 2018

requirement of sectoral coherence and therefore would fall outside the agricultural domain.

3.2 How to Measure Prevalence: Quantity vs. Value

The Italian Revenue Agency, in Circular No. 44/E of 2004, clarified how prevalence should be determined in practical terms[66]. When the products being compared are homogeneous (e.g., grapes from one's own farm vs. grapes purchased from others), the assessment must be made on a quantitative basis.

This interpretation has been upheld by the Italian Supreme Court (Corte di Cassazione) in a case involving a winery that grew high-quality grapes but used a larger volume of lower-quality grapes purchased externally for vinification. The Court ruled that, regardless of differences in quality or economic value, when products are of the same type, the test of prevalence is based exclusively on volume.

If the products are heterogeneous—such as different types of fruits or vegetables—then a comparison based on market value may be used instead.

3.3 When and What to Compare

The comparison must be made between the quantities (or values) of products effectively processed or manipulated by the agricultural entrepreneur, and not on the basis of overall sales or inventory.

For example, if a farm produces 10,000 kg of grapes and sells them directly to a cooperative without processing them, and in the same year purchases 5,000 kg of grapes from third parties and transforms them into wine, the prevalence requirement is not met—because only the third-party grapes were subject to transformation. As a result, the resulting wine would be treated as commercial income and not as agricultural income.

In principle, prevalence should be verified based on the products actually processed during the fiscal year. However, in some cases, the moment of sale may also be relevant, particularly where the connection to the farm's production is established only upon completion of the sale (i.e., the realization phase).

A good example is that of a red wine producer who buys white grapes to make white wine in order to diversify. In this case, to comply with the prevalence rule, it is advisable that the white wine be sold in the same year as the farm's own red wine production. This ensures that the internal benchmark for comparison—i.e.,

---

66 Italian Supreme Court (*Corte di Cassazione*), Order No. 18071 of 21 July 2017.

the self-produced red wine—has been effectively processed and placed on the market in the same fiscal period.

4. The "Franchise" Regime: Tolerance Margins in the Application of the Prevalence Criterion

While the **prevalence rule** is fundamental in distinguishing between agricultural income and business income under Italian tax law, the legislator has introduced a **flexibility mechanism**—commonly referred to as the ***"regime della franchigia"***—to account for minor deviations from strict compliance. This mechanism acknowledges the realities of agricultural production, where **seasonal variability, supply issues**, or **market demand** may occasionally require greater reliance on third-party products.

4.1 Legal Basis and Threshold of Tolerance

The franchise regime was introduced by Article 1, paragraph 423 of Law No. 311 of 30 December 2004 (the Finance Law for 2005), and later clarified by the Revenue Agency in Circular No. 44/E of 2004 and Resolution No. 50/E of 2011.

It provides that, in cases of minor excess, where the quantity of third-party products processed by the farm slightly exceeds its own production, the activity may still qualify as connected, albeit with partial tax consequences.

Specifically:

- The income derived from the third-party share that exceeds the farm's own production is excluded from the favorable agricultural tax regime;
- This portion is instead taxed as business income (***reddito d'impresa***), while the rest continues to benefit from the agricultural income classification.

4.2 An Example of Proportional Tax Treatment

Suppose a winery processes:

- 100 tonnes of grapes from its own vineyards, and
- 120 tonnes of grapes purchased from third parties.

The total processed is 220 tonnes, of which only 100 tonnes originate from the farm itself.

In this case, the wine produced from 100 tonnes qualifies as agricultural income, while the wine derived from the remaining 20 tonnes is taxed as business income.

This proportional attribution mechanism ensures that the entire activity is not reclassified simply due to a marginal overrun. At the same time, it discourages systematic or excessive reliance on third-party products, preserving the integrity of the agricultural status.

4.3 Limits of Applicability and Abuse Prevention

The franchise mechanism is designed for occasional or accidental deviations. If the prevalence of third-party products becomes structural or recurring, the tax authorities may reclassify the entire activity as business income, with significant implications in terms of taxation, accounting obligations, and VAT treatment.

Therefore, operators who wish to preserve their classification as agricultural enterprises must implement internal controls to monitor sourcing and processing volumes, and ensure that third-party inputs remain within acceptable limits—both in absolute and proportional terms.

5. Commercial Valorisation of Wine and Its Compatibility with the Legal Definition of Connected Agricultural Activity

Within the regulatory framework that defines connected agricultural activities, Italian law expressly includes the marketing and valorisation of agricultural products when carried out by the same entrepreneur who has cultivated or produced those goods. This is particularly relevant in the wine sector, where the quality and commercial positioning of the product depend not only on cultivation and transformation but also on branding, labelling, packaging, and communication strategies.

5.1 Marketing as a Legitimate Connected Activity

According to Article 2135(3) of the Civil Code and Article 32(2)(c) of the TUIR, the marketing of agricultural products may qualify as a connected activity as long as it concerns products primarily obtained through the entrepreneur's own agricultural operations.

This includes:

- Promotion of the farm's own brand;
- Distribution and direct sale of wine on national or foreign markets;
- Participation in trade fairs, exhibitions, and sectoral competitions;
- Use of quality labels, certifications, and designations of origin (PDO/PGI).

What matters is that these operations are functionally and economically linked to the transformation of the farm's own grapes into wine, thus remaining within the bounds of agricultural activity.

5.2 When Commercialisation Crosses the Line into Business Income

However, the mere act of marketing is not, in itself, sufficient to maintain the agricultural qualification. As noted by the Italian Revenue Agency and affirmed in relevant case law, if the wine sold has been:

- Entirely purchased from third parties, or
- Subject to no manipulation or transformation by the farm itself,

then the income generated from such marketing activities cannot be classified as agricultural income. It must instead be treated as business income (***reddito d'impresa***), governed by the rules of Article 55 TUIR.

This distinction is crucial in the wine sector, where the temptation to commercialise wines purchased from outside sources—perhaps to meet demand or expand offerings—is common. Agricultural enterprises must therefore take care to ensure that their commercial identity remains rooted in their own production.

5.3 Branding, Packaging, and Added Value

The inclusion of valorisation (***valorizzazione***) among the activities recognised as connected reflects the law's acknowledgement of the entrepreneurial dimension of modern agriculture.

In practice, this means that farms may lawfully invest in:

- Sophisticated packaging solutions;
- Graphic design and storytelling for labels;
- Strategic positioning of their wines in different market segments.

These efforts—far from being incompatible with the agricultural character of the enterprise—are considered fully legitimate, provided that they relate to products derived mainly from the farm's own raw materials.

5.4 The Strategic Role of Agricultural Law in Supporting Wine Enterprises

The evolution of the connected activity regime under Italian agricultural law, particularly in its application to the wine sector, demonstrates a deliberate legal effort to accompany and legitimise the growth of rural entrepreneurship. By recognizing processing, commercialisation, and valorisation as integral to agricultural identity—under the condition of prevalence and connection—the law fosters competitiveness without distorting tax neutrality.

For the modern winegrower, this represents both an opportunity and a responsibility: to innovate, promote, and expand, but always within the legal and structural framework of agricultural production.

The labelling of wine and wine products: nutrition declaration and health profiles

Ludovica Elena Asia Colombo,
*lawyer

Issues relating to the labelling of wine and wine products fall within the broader scope of European and national legislation on consumer information in the agri-food market.

Before delving into the core of the legislative innovations recently introduced on the labelling of wine products, it should be pointed out that the provisions laid down on the subject of food product information, which also includes wine products, are the result of a European policy aimed at pursuing the goals set out in Article 169 of the TFEU, such as the protection of the health, safety and economic interests of consumers, a protection that already outlined in Regulation (EU) No 1169/2011 on the provision of food information to consumers.

The aim of ensuring the right to information is pursued by the Legislator by identifying the adequacy of such information as a benchmark for the legitimacy of commercial communication. Preventing misleading actions or omissions that could deceive consumers regarding the characteristics of food products is intended to establish the relationship between producers and purchasers on the basis of the consumer's necessary awareness in making choices, thereby enabling them to make informed decisions affecting them.

In light of these considerations, the information provided on food product labelling constitutes one of the many forms of communication which, in the agri-food market, cannot be regarded as inherently free, neither in terms of content nor in the manner of its delivery, since it is nonetheless aimed at inducing those to whom it is addressed (consumers) to adopt a specific behaviour (namely, the act of purchasing), and must therefore be both impactful and effective.

Thus, in the agri-food market, communication does not merely fulfil an informational function, as is the case with communication in general, but is also vested with a cognitive function, which entails the need for the consumer not only to be informed, but also to be able to understand the data provided.

In this sense, the evolution of the rules governing the labelling of food products highlights how food information contributes not only to the functioning of the market, but also to safety, insofar as it concerns the circulation of wholesome and safe food.

Although, as mentioned above, Regulation (EU) No. 1169/2011 is the main source of legislation on the labelling of foodstuffs, the definition of which also includes wine products, it must be pointed out that for the wine sector, the law imposes special requirements identified by harmonisation rules of a vertical nature contained in Regulation (EU) No. 1308/2013 on the common organisation of agricultural markets (*i.e.* the "CMO" Regulation), now amended[67].

Indeed, while Regulation (EU) No 1169/2011, in Article 9, lists all the mandatory particulars to be included on the labels of agri-food products, and Article 36 merely outlines the general principles underlying such information, Articles 119 and 120 of the CMO Regulation set out, in both cases, the specific content of the particulars that must be expressly indicated on the labels of wines and wine products.

Specifically with regard to wine legislation, the adoption of the new Regulation (EU) No 2021/2117, approved as part of the 2023–2027 CAP reform, marked the first time that the European legislator intervened with substantial and significant amendments to the rules governing the labelling and presentation of wine products. These changes went beyond adjustments related to the production regime of quality wines and extended the informational obligations already applicable to food products also to wine and wine products, which had previously been exempt. Among these new obligations are the inclusion of the

67 This Regulation is the result of an extensive legislative process, as the wine sector was initially excluded from the single CMO Regulation set out in Regulation (EC) No 1234/2007, through which the legislator, in an effort to simplify the regulatory framework, undertook a revision of the European model for the regulation and governance of the agri-food sector. The following year, Regulation (EC) No 479/2008 on the wine CMO was adopted, whereby the European legislator brought together, in a single legal framework, the two core areas of market control and quality wines. The provisions of that Regulation were subsequently incorporated into the single CMO Regulation No 1234/2007 by Regulation (EC) No 491/2009. As part of the latest CAP reform, the CMO Regulation was further amended by Regulation (EU) No 2021/2117, which introduced changes to the system of authorisations for vine planting (Article 1, paragraphs 9–15) and to the PDO/PGI system for wines (Article 1, paragraphs 20–31).

list of ingredients and the nutritional declaration, as set out in Article 9, paragraph 1, letters (b) and (l) of Regulation (EU) No 1169/2011.

It is particularly worth noting that, prior to the adoption of the new Regulation, the legislative developments that traditionally shaped the wine sector reflected the classification of wine, especially its designation as a quality product, inasmuch as it is linked to a specific territory and therefore linked to specific geographical indications, whose legal protection has been considerably reinforced over time[68].

In light of the latest orientations of the European Commission—aimed at building a food system that "explores new ways" of informing consumers about food products—the legislator, likely driven by such objectives, has for the first time considered extending the aforementioned informational obligations also to wines and wine products, thereby enhancing the "educational" function of food information.

In order to understand this legislative choice—driven by the need to promote more informed purchasing decisions from a dietary and nutritional perspective, as well as its implications for consumer health—it is important to note that the new labelling obligations apply to the wine products listed in Annex VII, Part II of the CMO Regulation, including those that have been aromatised (see Regulation (EU) No 251/2014), such as:

a. wine, i.e. the product obtained exclusively from the total or partial alcoholic fermentation of fresh grapes, whether or not crushed, or of grape must;

b. new wine still in fermentation;

c. liqueur wine (with an actual alcoholic strength of not less than 15 % by volume and not more than 22 % by volume);

d. sparkling wine;

---

68 The relevant legislation includes: Regulation (EU) No 33/2019 of 17 October 2018, supplementing Regulation (EU) No 1308/2013 of the European Parliament and of the Council as regards applications for the protection of designations of origin, geographical indications and traditional terms in the wine sector, the opposition procedure, restrictions on use, amendments to product specifications, cancellation of protection, as well as labelling and presentation; Regulation (EU) 2023/1606 of 30 May 2023, amending Regulation (EU) 2019/33 as regards certain rules on the presentation of mandatory particulars for wine products and specific provisions on the indication and designation of ingredients in wine products; and Regulation (EU) 1143/2024 concerning the strengthening of quality schemes for wine products.

e. quality sparkling wine;

f. quality aromatic sparkling wine;

g. aerated sparkling wine;

h. semi-sparkling wine;

i. aerated semi-sparkling wine;

j. Grape must

k. Partially fermented grape must

l. Partially fermented grape must extracted from raisined grapes

m. Concentrated grape must

n. Rectified concentrated grape must

o. Wine from raisined grapes

p. Wine of overripe grapes

q. Wine vinegar, vinegar which: is obtained exclusively by acetous fermentation of wine and has a total acidity of not less than 60 grams per litre expressed as acetic acid.

r. Wine, quality sparkling wine, quality aromatic sparkling wine, aerated sparkling wine, semi-sparkling wine, aerated semi-sparkling wine (see point (1) and points (4) to (9) of Annex VII, Part II of Regulation (EU) No 1308/2013), which have undergone a process of total or partial dealcoholisation.

More specifically, the new Regulation has amended Article 119 of Regulation (EU) No 1308/2013 concerning compulsory labelling particulars, by establishing that the packaging or label of wine products must include the following mandatory indications:

I. The designation of the category of the wine product, in accordance with Annex VII, Part II, including, where applicable, the terms "dealcoholised" or "partially dealcoholised";

II. For wines with a protected designation of origin or protected geographical indication: *(i)* the expression "protected designation of origin" or "protected geographical indication"; and (ii) the name of the protected designation of origin or the protected geographical indication;

III. The actual alcoholic strength by volume;

IV. The indication of origin;

V. The name of the bottler, or in the case of sparkling wine, carbonated sparkling wine, quality sparkling wine or aromatised quality sparkling wine, the name of the producer or vendor;

VI. The name of the importer, in the case of imported wines;

VII. For sparkling wine, carbonated sparkling wine, quality sparkling wine or aromatised quality sparkling wine, the indication of the sugar content;

VIII. The nutrition declaration pursuant to Article 9(1)(l) of Regulation (EU) No 1169/2011;

IX. The list of ingredients pursuant to Article 9(1)(b) of Regulation (EU) No 1169/2011;

X. In the case of wine products that have undergone dealcoholisation in accordance with Annex VIII, Part I, Section E, and which have an actual alcoholic strength by volume of less than 10%, the minimum durability date pursuant to Article 9(1)(f) of Regulation (EU) No 1169/2011.

With regard to the nutrition declaration, the law also provides that it may be limited, on the packaging or on a label affixed to it, to the energy value alone. This may be expressed using the symbol "E" (energy) and must appear on the label in the same field of vision as the other mandatory particulars. In such cases, the full nutrition declaration may be provided by electronic means, by indicating a reference on the packaging or on a label affixed to it.

On this point, the European Commission, in its Communication of 24 November 2023, further clarified that the nutrition declaration and the list of ingredients may be provided by electronic means. The link—whether a QR code or a similar type of code—must appear on the label within the same field of vision as the other mandatory particulars. Moreover, the QR code or alternative barcode shown on the label must be accompanied by a clear reference to the type of information being made available electronically (therefore, at a minimum, the explicit terms "*Ingredients*" and "*Nutrition declaration*"). The mere use of standard symbols such as the information icon "*i*" is not considered appropriate for this purpose, although, incidentally, such symbols would have had the advantage of not requiring translation.

As a general rule, these new mandatory particulars shall apply to wines placed on the market from the date of application laid down in Regulation (EU) 2021/2117, namely 8 December 2023. However, wines "produced" before that date may continue to be placed on the market in accordance with the labelling requirements applicable prior to 8 December 2023, until stocks are exhausted.

In this regard, it should be noted that the Italian legislator has introduced certain corrective measures to the above provision on the labelling and marketing of aromatised wine products circulated within national territory. These products may bear labels displaying the ISO 2760 symbol "*i*" alongside the QR code referring to information on the list of ingredients and the nutrition declaration, until 30 June 2024. If not used by that date, the remaining labels may continue to be used only if corrected by applying a sticker bearing the word "*ingredients*" next to the "*i*" symbol, along with any other relevant indication. (see Ministerial Decree No. 115268 of 8 March 2024). In the event of non-compliance with these legal provisions, an administrative fine ranging from EUR 250 to EUR 5,000 shall apply (see Article 74(1) of Law No. 238/2016).

In light of the legislation outlined above, it is clear that the extension of such informational obligations to wine products represents a novelty within wine law, which has long been subject to significant regulatory developments concerning the protection of geographical indications for wines—starting from Regulations (EU) No 33/2019 and No 34/2019 up to the most recent Regulation (EU) No 1143/2024, aimed at strengthening all agri-food productions that exhibit characteristics, qualities or reputations linked to their place of origin[69].

In this context, the new requirements introduced under the reformed CAP regarding the nutrition declaration and the list of ingredients appear to be consistent with the objectives recently pursued by the European Union, as set out in the Communication of 20 May 2020 establishing the "Farm to Fork" Strategy. Framed within the broader European Green Deal, this strategy aims to implement a threefold sustainability approach across the entire food chain. The same applies to the Europe's Beating Cancer Plan of 2 February 2021. These two initiatives, taken together, promote consumer support in making "*healthy and sustainable*" food choices through tools—also digital ones—designed to

69 With regard to the new provisions on the labelling of products bearing geographical indications, and in order to enhance producer visibility, the Regulation introduces an obligation for agricultural products to indicate, on the label and within the same field of vision as the geographical indication, the name of the producer or of the operator—understood as the person responsible for the production phase or for the substantial transformation of the product. As regards spirit drinks, the Regulation requires that the name of the producer be indicated on the label (Article 37). Agricultural products and spirit drinks marketed under a geographical indication and labelled before 14 May 2026 may continue to be placed on the market without meeting the requirement to display the name of the producer or operator within the same field of vision as the geographical indication, until existing stocks are exhausted.

provide detailed information on the "*origin, nutritional value and environmental impact of food*"[70].

Indeed, the introduction of the obligation to include the nutrition declaration on the label of wine products is consistent with the view of the national legislator, according to which such a declaration is considered the most appropriate tool to inform consumers about the dietary impact of their consumption choices, thereby making those choices more conscious and aligned with the public health objectives pursued by the European Union (see point 2.3 of the Farm to Fork Strategy), including the reduction of harmful alcohol consumption, which forms an integral part of the Europe's Beating Cancer Plan.

However, the regulatory solutions adopted under Regulation (EU) No 2021/2117 present weaknesses that should not be underestimated, particularly with regard to the modalities for providing the new information required for wines. Indeed, although the new CAP appears to seek to fill a protection gap left by the horizontal framework on food information—namely Regulation (EU) No 1169/2011, which in Article 16(4) exempted alcoholic beverages from the obligation to bear such information on the label—the impression is that the new rules, in attempting to safeguard "health" and "sustainable lifestyles", end up imposing the provision of information to consumers that, in addition to being extremely technical, may also prove difficult to access.

In this respect, the newly introduced measures raise questions that had already been posed by Regulation (EU) No 1169/2011, particularly concerning the limits of the educational function assigned to business-to-consumer communication in the food sector. They also prompt some reflections on the objectives pursued by the legislator in this domain.

It is necessary to consider, on a case-by-case basis, whether the increasing informational burdens placed on producers respond not only to the interest shown by the majority of consumers in acquiring such knowledge, but also to the principles of subsidiarity, proportionality and sustainability that guide and shape the system. It is clear that the proliferation of mandatory information—particularly when highly technical—risks not only increasing costs for producers, with such costs likely to be passed on to the product, but also confusing consumers, thereby undermining their ability to make informed choices. In some cases, consumers may focus on nutritional data while

70 See COM(2019) 640 final of 11 December 2019, Communication from the Commission to the European Parliament, the European Council, the Council, the European Economic and Social Committee and the Committee of the Regions, the European Green Deal, point 2.1.6.

neglecting key elements necessary for proper interpretation. These considerations must also be assessed in light of the general principles of fairness set out in Article 7 of Regulation (EU) No 1169/2011, which—as is well known—provides a non-exhaustive list of requirements that food information must meet in order to be deemed "fair". These include not only truthfulness and non-misleading content, but also accuracy, clarity and comprehensibility. The notion of fairness also clearly encompasses the accessibility and intelligibility of food information—an aspect of particular relevance in the case of nutrition labelling and ingredient lists for wine, given that the legislator has, in an innovative way, allowed for such information to be provided to consumers in digital form.

Another issue that deserves attention is that, in addition to the obligation to include the nutrition declaration and the list of ingredients for wine products, the European Union—within the framework of the new "Europe's Beating Cancer Plan"—has set the objective of introducing specific "health warnings" on the labels of "alcoholic" products, with no distinction between wine and spirits. Along the same lines, Ireland has adopted the Public Health (Alcohol) Act, officially signed by the Minister for Health, Stephen Donnelly, on 22 May 2023. According to this legislation, starting from 10 January 2025, it will be mandatory, under Irish law, to include on the labels of "alcoholic products", in addition to the calorie content and the number of grams of alcohol per product, warnings intended to inform the public of the dangers of alcohol consumption during pregnancy and of the direct link between alcohol and cancer.

From this perspective, given that the European Union has not yet issued an official position, it should be noted that, although the nutrition declaration and health warnings are based on the assumption that there is a sort of automatic link between the provision of certain information, its reading by consumers, and the resulting adoption of informed and appropriate choices, alcoholic products are already perceived by the majority of consumers as not exactly "healthy" foods—regardless of whether health warnings or nutritional (and ingredient) information are provided.

This consideration does not seem entirely unrelated to the rationale ultimately followed by the European legislator in imposing the new informational obligations. In fact, Recital (42) of Regulation (EU) No 2021/2117, in outlining the reasons for introducing nutrition labelling and the list of ingredients for wines, does not explicitly mention the objective of facilitating the adoption by consumers of informed choices that would support a reduction in harmful alcohol consumption, in line with the "Europe's Beating Cancer Plan". Instead, it merely states that consumers should receive "more information". The vague and general nature of the wording used in Recital (42) may reflect the legislator's perceived difficulty in achieving effective outcomes in terms of consumers adopting nutritionally and dietetically sound choices that align with the Union's public health objectives.

Moreover, it should also be noted that such laconic wording is also present in the provisions of Regulation (EC) No 1924/2006 on nutrition and health claims made on foods. In particular, pursuant to Article 4 of that Regulation, the Commission was to establish, "by 19 January 2009", specific nutrient profiles, including exemptions, to be complied with by foods or certain categories of foods in order to bear nutrition or health claims, as well as the conditions for the use of such claims in relation to the nutrient profiles. However, this procedure has never been implemented.

The development of measures such as those adopted by Ireland—including, by way of example, supplementary forms of expression of the nutritional characteristics of food (see Article 35 of Regulation (EU) No 1169/2011), such as the French Nutriscore or Italy's NutrInform Battery—whose application remains highly debated and has significant implications for free competition in the market, are the consequence of a regulatory gap left by the European Union regarding the indication of the above-mentioned nutrient profiles. A harmonised EU-level framework would have ensured the introduction of a single European tool for the nutritional assessment of foods.

The use of labels developed on the basis of non-harmonised criteria may serve evidently protectionist purposes with respect to the importation of high-quality foreign products which, due to their nutritional characteristics, may be classified as "less healthy" and thereby infringe the principle of free movement of goods. Likewise, the introduction of health warnings conveying to consumers information that goes beyond mere health claims—warnings which, insofar as they relate to alcohol abuse, should not fall within the scope of the Regulation[71]—could be regarded as statements aimed at restricting trade between Member States, as they are driven by dissuasive rather than educational intentions, and could also significantly impact producers from a sanctions perspective.

For this reason, given that the European Commission has not yet adopted any official document aimed at regulating these aspects, it should be recalled that the

71 See Recital (10) of Regulation (EC) No 1924/2006.

boundary between the need to provide consumers with the most comprehensive possible information and the risk of diverting from the objectives laid down in the relevant EU provisions is extremely thin—particularly in light of the importance of quality wine products and their connection to their geographical area of production.

Wine Tourism in Italy: Legal Framework, Fiscal Profiles and Sustainable Development Perspectives

Fracesco Tedioli

*** Agricultural Law Expert Attorney, independent arbitrator and Adjunct Professor of Commercial law at the University of Mantova (Italy).**

Table of Contents:

1. Context, Opportunities, and Legal Framework

Wine tourism has emerged in recent years as one of the most promising avenues for the sustainable revitalisation of rural areas and the repositioning of the Italian wine industry in a context of global consumption decline. According to data presented at the XI Wine Monitor Forum by Nomisma, after the sharp contraction in global wine consumption recorded in 2023, the year 2024 confirmed the negative trend, with a -2% reduction in purchases in the large-scale retail channel in Italy. This decline, mainly due to inflation and the ageing of the domestic consumer base, contrasts with the expansion of exports in emerging markets such as Eastern Europe and Latin America.

In this framework, wine tourism offers an innovative response to the structural challenges of the wine sector, shifting the focus from product consumption to experiential value. As recent studies show[72], an increasing number of consumers, particularly in younger age groups, prefer immersive experiences at wineries over the traditional purchase of wine. The percentage of Italian tourists visiting wine-producing areas has risen from 60% in 2021 to 77% in 2025, signalling an important shift in the tourism paradigm.

72 Pedrabissi - Vasta, *Wine Tourism in Italy: A Virtuous and Sustainable Paradigm?*, in *Wine Tourism: A Legal Perspective, Tourism Law Review, n. 204/2022*, 2022, pp. 157–171.

This chapter provides an in-depth analysis of the legal, fiscal and policy dimensions of wine tourism in Italy. After an overview of the regulatory framework introduced by Law No. 205/2017 and the Ministerial Decree of 12 March 2019, the analysis will address the legal classification of wine tourism as a connected agricultural activity, the fiscal implications under Italian law, the evolution of regional legislation, and the broader socio-economic impact of wine tourism as a lever for territorial development and cultural valorisation.

The discussion is enriched with doctrinal and statistical references, including international comparisons with France and Spain, and integrates key findings from the literature[73] to underline the potential of wine tourism as a virtuous model of sustainable and integrated rural tourism.

2. The Rise of Wine Tourism in Italy: Socioeconomic Relevance and Cultural Evolution

Over the past decade, wine tourism has emerged as a significant strategic lever for revitalizing the Italian wine industry and promoting sustainable development in rural areas. In the wake of a global downturn in wine consumption—confirmed by the 2024 Wine Monitor report, which recorded a -2% contraction in domestic sales through large-scale distribution channels—the search for alternative models of growth has intensified. The sector has responded by pivoting toward experiential tourism, transforming wine from a commodity into a cultural interface between production and territory.

The data support this evolution: according to Roberta Garibaldi, president of the Italian Association for Food and Wine Tourism, Italian wine tourists increased from 60% of total food tourists in 2021 to over 77% in 2025. This shift reflects a growing desire among consumers to engage directly with wine regions through immersive activities—visiting wineries, participating in harvests, and learning about local designations and practices.

Notably, this experiential transformation has also spurred institutional responses. For the first time in 2025, *Vinitaly* hosted a dedicated "Vinitaly Tourism" pavilion featuring over sixty wineries, international tour operators, and dedicated B2B events, underscoring the growing synergies between viticulture and tourism in Italy. The aim is not only to capitalize on tourist flows, but also to reposition wine regions as "destinations," thereby multiplying the indirect benefits for territorial economies.

73 Pedrabissi – Vasta, cit.; Garibaldi, *Rapporto sul Turismo Enogastronomico Italiano 2021*, Ed. Associazione Italiana Turismo Enogastronomico, Milano, 2021; Cappelletto, *Enoturismo in Italia. Profili giuridici, fiscali e gestionali*, Milano, 2020..

In legal terms, wine tourism is no longer a nebulous or ancillary activity. Since the inclusion of its definition in Article 1, paragraph 502 of Law No. 205/2017 (Budget Law 2018), Italian legislation has formally recognized wine tourism as a specific category of activity. This includes all forms of wine knowledge carried out in situ: guided visits to vineyards and cellars, educational initiatives, and the direct marketing of wines—even in combination with food tastings and local gastronomic offerings.

The regulatory framework was later enriched by the Ministerial Decree of March 12, 2019, which established the *Guidelines and quality standards for wine tourism activities*. This decree clarified that wine tourism constitutes an ancillary agricultural activity under Article 2135 of the Italian Civil Code, provided it is carried out by an agricultural entrepreneur. The decree further detailed the requirements for facilities, hygiene and safety standards, multilingual informational materials, and staff training—essentially codifying the infrastructural and organizational prerequisites for the modern wine tourist experience.

The relevance of wine tourism, however, is not limited to its economic dimension. The sector serves as a powerful instrument of territorial valorization, combining cultural heritage, environmental stewardship, and local identity. Through this lens, wine tourism becomes a paradigmatic form of "gentle mobility," reinforcing the bonds between sustainability, landscape conservation, and slow travel practices. It is no coincidence that many wineries now integrate architecture, art, and landscape design into their hospitality offerings—a model championed by initiatives such as *Toscana Wine Architecture*.

In conclusion, wine tourism represents more than a niche segment of the wine market; it is a multidisciplinary and cross-sectoral phenomenon that binds together law, culture, economy, and ecology. Its continued growth calls for coordinated governance, including urban planning tools, fiscal incentives, and investment in soft infrastructure—such as digital booking systems and sustainable mobility networks—that can help position Italy not only as a producer of excellent wines, but also as a global leader in immersive wine-based tourism.

3. Sustainability and Regulatory Innovation in Wine Tourism

The concept of sustainability—long viewed as an aspirational principle—has in recent years acquired the normative stature of a legal cornerstone, particularly within the European Union's policy framework. This shift has been accelerated by the advent of the European Green Deal, which promotes not only ecological transition but also social inclusion and territorial cohesion. The Green Deal articulates an ambitious vision: to transform Europe into a just and prosperous society by adopting a regenerative economy model that reconciles environmental protection with productivity. This transformation is predicated on the recognition that economic growth must be decoupled from environmental degradation—a paradigm shift that redefines the role of sustainability from a mere principle to a concrete objective in policy-making[74].

This framework has also reshaped the regulatory approach to tourism. No longer conceived as a neutral sector of economic relevance, tourism—particularly wine tourism—is now understood as a tool for territorial valorisation and cultural regeneration. Within this context, wine tourism is ideally positioned to align with the goals of the circular economy, thanks to its inherent ability to link agricultural production with environmental stewardship and cultural identity.

Indeed, wine tourism offers a compelling model of "attentive and conscious" tourism, where economic and environmental interests converge. It promotes resource-efficient activities with low ecological impact, while contributing to local development and social inclusion, particularly in rural and marginalised areas. The emphasis on sustainability has also influenced legal interpretations, bringing the notion of "territorial governance" to the fore. In this vision, planning and regulatory interventions are no longer top-down directives but instruments that derive their legitimacy from a polycentric and multilevel governance approach—one that includes local communities, regional governments, and national institutions[75].

What emerges is a legal architecture that repositions wine tourism within a broader ethical and political project. In this architecture, sustainability is not just a requirement for environmental protection, but a normative principle that calls for administrative simplification, economic inclusion, and the cultural promotion of place-based identities. As the doctrine has rightly observed, this evolution leads to a regulatory space where different legal domains—agriculture, tourism,

74 Pedrabissi, *Il trasporto aereo nazionale nel Piano Nazionale di Ripresa e Resilienza*, in *RQDA*; see also Fracchia, *Il principio dello sviluppo sostenibile*, in *Studi sui principi del diritto amministrativo*, 2012, p. 433

75 See Cecchetti, *La revisione degli artt. 9 e 41 della Costituzione*, in *Forum Quad. Cost.*, 2021, p. 285; De Leonardis, *L'ambiente tra i principi fondamentali della costituzione*, in *Federalismi.it*, 3/2004

environment, and culture—intersect and where the wine territory becomes both the object and the subject of sustainable development policies[76].

4. The Legal Definition of Wine Tourism in Italian Law

The legal recognition of wine tourism in Italy is relatively recent. For a long time, the phenomenon remained outside any formal normative classification, despite its growing relevance for the Italian agricultural and tourism sectors. A turning point occurred with the enactment of Law No. 205 of 27 December 2017 (the so-called *Legge di Bilancio 2018*), which introduced for the first time an express legal definition of wine tourism. According to Article 1, paragraph 502 of the law, "wine tourism" includes all activities aimed at increasing knowledge of wine conducted at the place of production, encompassing visits to vineyards and wineries, displays of viticultural tools, guided tastings, and the sale of the company's wines, including in combination with food, as well as educational and recreational initiatives within wine cellars.

This legislative innovation was implemented through the Ministerial Decree of 12 March 2019, issued by the Ministry of Agriculture and the Ministry of Tourism. The decree set out the *Guidelines and directions on the minimum quality standards required for the exercise of wine tourism*, thereby creating a uniform regulatory framework for the entire national territory. Most notably, the decree clarified that wine tourism is to be legally classified as a *connected agricultural activity* under Article 2135, paragraph 3 of the Italian Civil Code. This classification allows winemakers—individually or collectively organised—to conduct wine tourism activities under the same legal regime applicable to their agricultural operations, thus facilitating simplified tax and administrative treatment.

From a fiscal standpoint, wine tourism benefits from the preferential tax regime established for agritourism activities under Article 5 of Law No. 413 of 30 December 1991. The decree also provided a detailed list of activities that fall within the scope of wine tourism, including visits to vineyards and cellars, tastings of wines produced on site (possibly paired with typical regional foods), and educational, cultural, or recreational initiatives such as workshops and harvest experiences (*vendemmia didattica*).

Importantly, the regulatory framework emphasizes the territorial dimension of wine tourism. Activities must be connected to the regional wine production

76 Vasta, *Uso turistico del territorio*, in *Amministrazione pubblica e mercato del turismo*, 2012

system, with particular attention to products with geographical indications (DOP, IGP). The food products served during tastings must predominantly come from local supply chains and respect sanitary standards, without transforming the wine tasting experience into a restaurant service—thus maintaining its agricultural character.

Wine tourism providers must also meet a number of quality standards, including offering visits at least three days a week (including weekends and holidays), providing online booking systems, making available multilingual promotional materials, and employing trained personnel familiar with the region's history and enogastronomic identity. The decree entrusts Italy's Regions with the task of overseeing operator training and monitoring compliance with the law, while municipalities manage the authorisation process through the SCIA procedure (*Segnalazione Certificata di Inizio Attività*).

This regulatory evolution responds to the need to reposition wine tourism within a framework of public interest, as a tool for the enhancement of rural areas and the diversification of agricultural income sources. The legal classification of wine tourism as a connected agricultural activity is crucial to this aim, as it anchors such activities to the multifunctionality of the agricultural enterprise—a concept widely promoted by European and Italian agricultural policy since the early 2000s[77]

By finally providing legal certainty, the 2019 decree and its implementing acts have made it possible for Italian wine tourism to evolve from an informal practice into a legally structured sector, capable of attracting investments, fostering quality improvements, and stimulating regional development. Nevertheless, differences in implementation across Italy's regions remain a challenge, calling for greater harmonisation and strategic coordination among local authorities.

5. Regional Regulations and Implementation Challenges

Following the adoption of the 2019 Ministerial Decree, the responsibility for concretely implementing wine tourism regulations was devolved to the Italian Regions, in accordance with the principle of subsidiarity that governs the division of competences in matters of agriculture and tourism. Each Region was tasked with defining the procedural and operational details required for authorising and monitoring wine tourism activities, including the adoption of specific SCIA (Certified Notification of Start of Activity) forms, the

77 Cappelletto, *L'agricoltura multifunzionale*, 2020, pp. 19–23.

identification of competent authorities, and the establishment of minimum requirements.

However, the implementation process across Italy has been fragmented and uneven, reflecting the broader asymmetries that characterise Italian regionalism. While some Regions acted promptly—for instance, Lombardy was the first to issue an implementing decree on 22 October 2019—others took years to adopt adequate legislation. Notably, Campania approved a regional wine tourism law only in December 2024, significantly delaying the practical applicability of the national framework in its territory.

These delays have hindered the uniform development of the wine tourism sector, creating disparities in the accessibility of the activity across regional borders. The absence of shared procedural models has not only slowed down the growth of wine tourism but also caused confusion among operators and local administrations, especially regarding the requirements for authorisation and compliance with health and safety standards.

Moreover, some Regions have expanded the legal framework, introducing additional obligations and supervisory mechanisms. Tuscany, for instance, approved amendments to its regional agritourism law (Law No. 30/2003) in November 2019, explicitly integrating wine tourism into the broader system of rural hospitality. These measures established new minimum standards for facilities and staff training and reinforced the linkage between wine tourism and the promotion of DOP and IGP products.

Despite these efforts, significant implementation challenges persist. Among the most critical is the need for adequate transport infrastructure and digital tools that can support booking, communication, and integrated service delivery. As highlighted in recent reports, wine tourists increasingly seek immersive experiences that combine authenticity, accessibility, and storytelling. Yet in many rural areas, basic services such as signage, public transport connections, or multilingual guides are still lacking.

To overcome these obstacles, a systemic approach is required—one that involves coordinated action among stakeholders at different institutional levels, from municipal administrations to regional tourism boards and national agencies for the promotion of Italian wine. Without such a concerted effort, the full potential of wine tourism—as a lever for rural development and for the revitalisation of Italy's inner areas—will remain underexploited.

6. Economic Impact and International Comparisons

The economic relevance of wine tourism in Italy has grown substantially over the last decade, evolving from a niche practice into a pillar of territorial marketing and rural development. According to data collected by Città del Vino, the total number of visitors to Italian wine tourism destinations was estimated at approximately 14 million in 2018, including both overnight tourists and day trippers, with an overall turnover of roughly €2.5 billion. This economic magnitude underscores the strategic importance of the sector not only for individual wineries but for the national economy as a whole.

From a comparative perspective, Italy's wine tourism system shows both strengths and areas for improvement when measured against other European wine-producing countries. France, for instance, recorded around 10 million wine tourists in 2016, with 42% of them coming from abroad, and a total business volume of €5.2 billion. The upward trajectory has been particularly marked among international tourists, with a 40% increase from 2009 to 2016. Spain, although relying on more limited data—mostly from wineries associated with the Rutas del Vino—reported 2.1 million wine tourists in 2018 across 595 wineries open to the public, showing a positive trend and a 19% increase compared to the previous year.

These comparisons highlight both the vitality of the wine tourism sector across Europe and the competitive pressure that Italian operators face in positioning themselves in the international market. While Italy offers unmatched oenological diversity and a deeply rooted viticultural heritage, it still lags behind France in terms of foreign wine tourist attraction and behind Spain in terms of structured itineraries and integrated promotion systems. The absence of a coherent national strategy for wine tourism and the lack of a unified platform for booking and promotion may be partly responsible for this competitive gap.

The strengths of Italian wine tourism lie primarily in the quality and variety of the offer. With over 526 DOP and IGP wines and a production value of €8.9 billion[78], Italy is a global leader in high-quality wine. The challenge, however, is to translate this excellence into coordinated territorial experiences capable of attracting and retaining visitors. Here, the integration of wine tourism with other forms of cultural and environmental tourism—such as food trails, UNESCO heritage sites, and rural festivals—can prove decisive.

---

78 Cf. Ismea-*Qualivita*, 2018.

Furthermore, the sustainability dimension is gaining prominence. New generations of tourists increasingly demand responsible and regenerative experiences. As noted by Garibaldi (2021), wine tourism today is no longer just about tasting but about engaging with local culture, understanding production methods, and contributing to the preservation of landscapes and traditions.

In this context, wine tourism emerges not only as a commercial tool but as a transformative force capable of revitalising peripheral areas, promoting social cohesion, and enhancing the reputation of wine territories on a global scale. To realise its full potential, however, sustained investment in infrastructure, digital innovation, staff training, and territorial governance remains indispensable.

7. Between Crisis and Innovation: The Strategic Role of Wine Tourism in the Italian Wine Sector

Wine tourism represents a valuable opportunity for the revitalisation of rural and inner areas, the diversification of farm income, and the enhancement of cultural and territorial heritage. In the Italian context, despite certain infrastructural and administrative challenges, the legal recognition of wine tourism—most notably through Law No. 205/2017 and the Ministerial Decree of 12 March 2019—has laid the groundwork for a structured regulatory framework capable of fostering sustainable and high-quality development of the sector.

The national legal framework defines wine tourism not merely as a commercial activity, but as an "agricultural ancillary activity"[79] , thereby integrating it within the multifunctional model of agriculture endorsed by the EU and Italian institutions. The provisions adopted at regional level—albeit still fragmented and uneven—reflect an increasing awareness of the economic, social, and environmental potential of this activity. Regions such as Lombardy, Tuscany, and Campania have started to implement specific legislation, addressing procedural requirements, quality standards, and coordination with local tourism policies.

From a policy perspective, the integration of wine tourism within broader territorial strategies—such as rural development plans, protected geographical indication systems, and cultural routes—can significantly amplify its impact. Consumers increasingly seek immersive and meaningful experiences that connect wine with its place of origin, its production culture, and its human dimension. This "experiential turn" in consumer behaviour aligns perfectly with

79 *Ex* Art. 2135, para. 3, Italian Civil Code.

the potentialities of wine tourism as a tool for territorial branding and local identity promotion.

Nevertheless, the full realisation of wine tourism's potential requires the resolution of several critical issues: logistical and infrastructural gaps, lack of integration between the various actors of the supply chain, limited training of personnel, and persistent regulatory asymmetries across regional borders. Furthermore, the sustainability of wine tourism initiatives must be ensured, both from an environmental and socio-economic standpoint, avoiding forms of overexploitation and commercial homogenisation that risk undermining the authenticity of the territories involved.

In this regard, the role of professional operators, local administrations, and protection consortia is crucial in ensuring compliance with standards, promoting synergies between actors, and designing tourism products that are consistent with the identity and resources of the local wine landscape. If adequately supported by public policies and private investment, wine tourism can become a paradigm of virtuous and resilient development, capable of enhancing the Italian wine sector not only in terms of production, but also in terms of cultural and territorial innovation.

The Legal and Operational Role of Customs Codes in the International Trade of Italian Wine

Fracesco Tedioli
*** Agricultural Law Expert Attorney, independent arbitrator and Adjunct Professor of Commercial law at the University of Mantova (Italy).**

Table of Contents:

1. Customs Classification and Export Compliance in the Italian Wine Sector

Italy stands among the world's leading wine exporters, a position built upon centuries of tradition, varietal diversity, and a strong reputation for quality. However, in today's global marketplace, excellence in product alone does not suffice. To successfully compete in foreign markets, wineries must navigate an intricate web of legal norms, technical requirements, and customs constraints. In this context, the customs classification of wine—commonly referred to as the Harmonized System (HS) Code—emerges as a pivotal yet often overlooked element in the export strategy.

The HS Code is a numerical identifier used globally to classify goods in international trade. It plays a decisive role in determining applicable customs duties, verifying compliance with sanitary or phytosanitary regulations, compiling trade statistics, enforcing restrictions or bans, and granting access to preferential tariff treatments under bilateral or multilateral agreements. As such, understanding and properly applying the customs code for wine is not merely a bureaucratic necessity, but a competitive advantage in export operations.

2. Structure of the HS Code and Classification Challenges

Within the European Union, customs classification is regulated through the Combined Nomenclature (CN), which integrates the internationally harmonized system into the EU legal framework. The first six digits of the code, known as the HS code, identify the essential characteristics of the product and are standardized globally. These can be extended to eight or ten digits within the EU's TARIC (Integrated Tariff of the European Union) system to capture more detailed specifications for customs purposes.

For wine, the classification depends on several variables, including the type of wine (still, sparkling, fortified), the alcohol content, packaging, and sometimes the presence of a protected designation of origin. The primary HS codes used for wine include 2204.10 for sparkling wines, 2204.21 for still wines with an alcohol content not exceeding 14% vol., and 2204.29 for those exceeding 14% vol. Wines with specific characteristics or packaging formats may be subject to additional subdivisions within the TARIC system.

A misclassification—even by a single digit—can result in significant consequences. For example, applying an incorrect code to a DOP-certified wine such as *Brunello di Montalcino* may lead to overpayment of duties or the loss of preferential access granted under free trade agreements. In more severe cases, the incorrect classification could trigger shipment delays, customs fines, or outright refusals at the destination border. This is particularly true for bulk wine exports, which are often confused with bottled wine when the proper packaging indicators are not used.

Given these risks, customs compliance must be treated as a strategic function, requiring technical precision and legal awareness. Exporting wine is not simply a matter of logistics—it is an operation embedded in a multilayered regulatory framework that demands attention to detail and proactive risk management.

3. Preferential Trade Agreements and Proof of Origin

One of the most significant advantages offered by accurate customs classification is access to preferential tariff treatments under bilateral or multilateral trade agreements. The European Union has signed numerous Free Trade Agreements (FTAs) with third countries—such as Japan, Canada (CETA), and South Korea—that reduce or eliminate import duties on goods originating in the EU. For Italian wine exporters, this translates into tangible economic benefits, especially in highly competitive markets.

To benefit from preferential tariffs, exporters must be able to prove the preferential origin of their products in accordance with the rules of origin specified in each agreement. This generally entails demonstrating that the wine has been entirely produced within the EU, including all relevant stages such as vinification and bottling, and that it complies with any additional conditions set by the importing country.

Proper origin documentation typically includes the use of origin declarations on invoices by registered exporters (REX system), or the issuance of EUR.1 movement certificates validated by customs authorities. These documents must be retained and presented upon request during customs inspections, both in the EU and in the destination country.

Failing to comply with origin requirements can have serious consequences. A wine that is otherwise eligible for duty-free treatment may be subjected to full import tariffs if the proof of origin is deemed insufficient. Moreover, inaccurate or false declarations may lead to administrative penalties or exclusion from future preferential access.

Thus, understanding the interplay between HS classification and rules of origin is essential for ensuring full compliance with international trade law and for safeguarding the competitive position of Italian wine on global markets. The complexity of these requirements underscores the need for a robust internal compliance structure, capable of tracking product origin, maintaining supporting documentation, and keeping up with frequent regulatory updates.

4. Customs Documentation and Logistical Planning

The successful export of wine does not conclude with its classification or compliance with origin rules—it also hinges on the meticulous preparation of customs documentation and the strategic coordination of logistics. Errors or omissions in this phase can result in delays, seizure of goods, or unnecessary financial burdens.

The cornerstone of customs documentation is the commercial invoice, which serves not only as a fiscal document but also as a descriptive summary for customs authorities. While standard invoice information includes the exporter and importer details, product description, quantity, and unit price, exporters are strongly advised to also include: 1) the correct customs code (HS/TARIC); 2) the origin of the product, and 3) the delivery terms (Incoterms® 2020).

Together, these elements provide clarity for customs officials in both the exporting and importing countries, ensuring proper application of duties and avoiding interpretive ambiguities. For instance, the distinction between wine exported in bulk and wine exported in bottles may affect applicable tariff lines and must be properly stated.

In parallel, logistics planning plays a critical role. Exporters must carefully choose the mode of transport (road, rail, sea, or air), taking into account cost, timing, and risk. The identification of appropriate customs clearance points—both at the point of exit from the EU and at the port of entry abroad—is fundamental. The shipment should be accompanied by a complete set of transport documents (such as the bill of lading or CMR waybill) and, where necessary, certificates of origin, analysis, or conformity, depending on the importing country's requirements.

Another crucial document is the Single Administrative Document (SAD), which serves as the EU customs declaration for the movement of goods both within and outside the Union. This must be filled out in accordance with the specifics of the shipment and submitted through the Customs Decision System (CDS), often by a customs broker or forwarding agent.

The Incoterms® used in the sales contract further influence customs responsibilities. For example, the use of DDP (Delivered Duty Paid) places the full burden of customs clearance, duties, and transportation costs on the exporter. Conversely, EXW (Ex Works) shifts these responsibilities to the importer. An accurate understanding and use of Incoterms® are thus essential for managing liability and cost allocation effectively.

All these components underscore the necessity for wineries engaged in export to adopt an integrated approach, coordinating commercial, legal, and logistical functions. Reliance on specialized customs consultants or freight forwarders can greatly reduce the risk of errors, but ultimate responsibility still rests with the exporter.

5. Digital Tools and Customs Databases: Enhancing Compliance and Efficiency

In the increasingly complex regulatory environment of international trade, digital tools and customs databases represent indispensable resources for wine exporters seeking to ensure compliance and reduce procedural risks. These platforms enable real-time access to updated information on customs classification, applicable duties, non-tariff measures, and required documentation.

The TARIC system (Integrated Tariff of the European Union), managed by the European Commission and accessible via the Italian Customs and Monopolies Agency (ADM), provides detailed data on all import and export measures applicable within the EU. Exporters can search for the correct customs code

(HS/TARIC) of their product, and verify specific conditions for entry into third countries—including import licenses, sanitary and phytosanitary (SPS) requirements, and anti-dumping duties.

For example, an exporter of Prosecco seeking to ship to the United States can use TARIC to determine the exact classification under code 2204.10.15 (sparkling wine), confirm that no prohibitions apply, and check if any preferential treatment is in force under the EU–US trade framework. These databases also provide details about documentation requirements such as certificates of origin, phytosanitary certificates, and EUR.1 movement certificates, which may be essential to benefit from tariff reductions under preferential agreements.

In addition to TARIC, the EU Access2Markets portal offers an intuitive interface for small and medium-sized enterprises. This platform enables exporters to navigate trade agreements and origin rules and to simulate customs duties by country and product. It also includes the ROSA (Rules of Origin Self-Assessment) tool, which assists operators in verifying whether their products meet the criteria for preferential origin.

On the Italian side, the ADM Customs Tariff Database provides similar functionalities, with additional support for the electronic submission of customs declarations via the Customs Decision System and Single Window platform, enabling more efficient coordination among different administrative bodies (e.g., veterinary services, health authorities, Ministry of Agriculture).

The adoption of such instruments is not merely a matter of operational convenience; it is a prerequisite for risk mitigation. Mistakes in classification or in the application of origin protocols can lead to retroactive recovery of duties, fines, or even criminal liability in cases of suspected customs fraud. Furthermore, incorrect documentation can cause delays, storage costs, and reputational harm, particularly in the context of highly regulated markets such as Canada, Japan, or the United States.

In conclusion, digital customs tools are critical not only for proper classification and compliance, but also for enhancing the efficiency and predictability of export operations. Their integration into internal export processes should be regarded as a best practice for all Italian wine producers operating in international markets.

6. Strategic Relevance of Customs Compliance in the Wine Export Sector

The success of Italian wine exports depends not only on the intrinsic quality and heritage of the product, but also on the capacity of operators to navigate a complex and evolving regulatory landscape. Among the various technical dimensions that influence international competitiveness, customs classification stands out as a strategic lever. The Harmonized System (HS) codes, together with the TARIC nomenclature and the preferential origin rules under bilateral and multilateral trade agreements, form a sophisticated framework that must be interpreted and applied with precision.

Incorrect application of customs codes, misclassification of goods, or failure to comply with origin documentation requirements can generate not only economic inefficiencies—such as overpayment of duties or loss of trade preferences—but also legal risks. This is particularly significant in sectors such as wine, where the value of exports is tightly linked to reputation, certification, and compliance with geographical indication (GI) regimes.

From an operational standpoint, the integration of digital tools, such as the TARIC system and Access2Markets, into company workflows represents a turning point. These platforms are not merely information repositories, but real instruments of governance for global supply chains. They facilitate real-time decision-making, allow for pre-emptive identification of risks, and ensure alignment with both EU and non-EU regulatory requirements.

Moreover, customs compliance extends beyond the moment of exportation. It affects contractual structuring (through Incoterms®), insurance coverage, fiscal optimization, and overall business planning. For this reason, Italian wine companies—especially SMEs—must adopt an integrated approach that combines technical knowledge of customs rules with proactive legal and commercial strategies.

In conclusion, the customs code of wine is far from a bureaucratic formality. It is a powerful operational and strategic tool that must be mastered in order to fully unlock the potential of Italian wines in international markets. A correct and efficient use of customs procedures enables companies not only to access foreign markets under the best conditions, but also to affirm the excellence and authenticity of their products in an increasingly competitive global arena.

www.ingramcontent.com/pod-product-compliance
Lightning Source LLC
LaVergne TN
LVHW022049200926
848481LV00003B/844
* 9 7 9 8 8 9 9 6 6 1 1 8 1 *